SCHOLASTIC

Mastering the 5-Paragraph Essay

by Susan Van Zile

NEW YORK • TORONTO • LONDON • AUCKLAND • SYDNEY
MEXICO CITY • NEW DELHI • HONG KONG • BUENOS AIRES

Teaching *Resources*

Acknowledgments

To the Great Creator who generously and lovingly bestows upon us all that we are and all that we have.

To my magnificent students who inspire me, teach me, and bring me great joy. Thank you for sharing your gifts and talents.

To my husband Phil, my children Caroline and Taylor, and my parents for their abiding love, support, understanding, and encouragement.

To my colleague Marilyn Breed and the ninth-grade team for sharing their creative ideas and wisdom.

To the administration, teachers, and students of the Cumberland Valley School District who have consistently provided me with a rich and rewarding academic environment in which to grow.

To Virginia Dooley and Terry Cooper for making my dreams come true.

To Scholastic for supporting and nurturing children.

Cover design by Adana Jimenez

Interior design by Sydney Wright

Interior photos courtesy of the author

ISBN 0-439-63525-X

Contents

✑ INTRODUCTION ✑

What's Inside and Why

Why Should Students Learn How to Write the Five-Paragraph Essay?

In today's world of national and state standards and the accountability demanded by the No Child Left Behind Act, students are often faced with high-stakes tests—tests that demand multiparagraph essays containing an introduction, a body, and a conclusion. One way to help students prepare for these assessments is by teaching them how to craft a five-paragraph essay. As an organizational framework, this type of essay is flexible enough to be used with various types of writing, including the narrative, informational (expository), and persuasive modes that are included on most state tests. The five-paragraph essay also provides an excellent vehicle for writing across the curriculum. It can be utilized in subjects ranging from science to social studies to even math. And it will serve students later on: The most recent version of the SAT includes a section that asks students to compose an organized, thoughtful, and well-written essay. Thus, to prepare students to face their real-life writing challenges, it is imperative to teach the five-paragraph essay.

Just as important as teaching students the structure of a well-conceived essay and providing ample practice for its mastery is the task of engaging students in meaningful writing activities that will help them develop and discover their special, unique voice. Because children learn to write through repeated practice, journaling for a few minutes each day can lead to stories, poems, fables, satire, and more. Reading examples not only of exquisite writing but also of humorous pieces can inspire students to produce excellent essays that are not formulaic in nature.

By linking students' prior knowledge of the paragraph to the concept of a fully developed essay, Chapter 1 demonstrates that the essay is simply an expanded version of the paragraph. Making this connection is essential if students are to store the information in their long-term memory. In addition, the chapter begins at the lowest level of Bloom's taxonomy, the knowledge level, introducing students to the terminology associated with the essay's structure. As partners build a model of a five-paragraph essay and take turns explaining the relationship between the parts of the model and the parts of the essay, they proceed to the comprehension level of Bloom's taxonomy. Throughout the text the concept of scaffolding is used: In graduated steps students move from simpler to more complex forms of essay writing. The model-building activity is also supported by the research of Carol Ann Tomlinson and M. Layne Kalbfleisch (1998), which states that "the brain learns best when it 'does' rather than absorbs."

Once students have a basic understanding of the structure of the five-paragraph essay, they can use this knowledge to construct informational, narrative, and persuasive essays. Because research proves that semantic information, such as the word knowledge inherent in essay writing, "must be repeatedly processed for long-term storage to take place" (Sprenger, 1999, p. 51), the same procedures, from webbing to editing checklists, are used to teach the informational, narrative, and persuasive modes of writing delineated in chapters 2–4. In addition, the thesis statement for each type of essay uses the three-point approach: It states the main idea or topic of the essay, provides the writer's opinion or point of view about the subject, and briefly outlines the topics of the three body paragraphs. When first introduced to this method of constructing a thesis statement, I was not convinced of its value. However, I am now a convert, for I have discovered that requiring students to use the three-point thesis greatly improves the focus, organization, and unity of their essay.

Chapter 5 introduces a cross-curricular application of the five-paragraph essay, including a model of a science essay comparing the praying mantis and the walking stick. Chapter 6, which focuses on the literary essay, explores the higher-order thinking skills of analysis, synthesis, and evaluation as students learn how to introduce appropriate quotations from the text into their writing. Because formal literary essays are more complex than the other types, I usually reserve these lessons for seventh, eighth, and ninth graders, although they can be easily adapted for younger students. In addition to providing models of various types of essays, this book also includes activities, revision strategies, editing sheets, and mini-lessons designed to help students improve their ability to write five-paragraph essays.

Although the five-paragraph essay is difficult to teach as well as to learn, most students are able to generate excellent essays when they are guided step-by-step through the process as well as given lots of opportunities for practice and revision. When one of my reluctant ninth-grade writers immediately began to generate a web for her midterm essay, I smiled broadly, and she remarked, "If I practice enough, I get it. Once I get it, I get it." This statement along with such comments as "We should have learned about the thesis statement earlier. Be sure you teach it to the eighth graders next year" demonstrate the value of the five-paragraph essay. However, nothing reinforces the success of my experience with the five-paragraph essay more clearly than the following comment from Dave, an eleventh grader who was repeating ninth-grade English. After he completed the eleventh-grade state writing assessment, he flew into my room and declared, "I nailed it, Mrs. Van Zile. I knew how to write the persuasive essay, and I had three reasons to support my position." He then chattered on about everything he had written, even though he had been the biggest and loudest opponent of the five-paragraph essay at the beginning of the school year.

Tips for Teaching the Five-Paragraph Essay

○ Model each step of the process and move students through each one slowly and gradually.

○ Proceed from informational, narrative, and persuasive essays to more complex forms.

○ Repeat the procedure used to teach the structure of the essay several times so students can internalize the process and store it in their long-term memories.

○ Once students have internalized the process for writing five-paragraph essays, vary the form and structure.

○ Engage students by including relevant topics and motivating activities. Allow them to work with partners or in groups, and vary the types of writing assignments.

C H A P T E R   1

*I*ntroducing the Five-Paragraph Essay

Background Information

What better way to introduce students to the five-paragraph essay than to begin with a topic they enjoy: heroes. In my class, we first read a nonfiction essay about Jackie Robinson called "Justice at Last" as well as an uplifting story called "A Firefighter's New Friend," in which a heroic child named Juliana donates all of her savings to the children of the firefighters who lost their lives on September 11. After making a list of the heroic qualities possessed by Robinson, Juliana, and the firefighters, I ask students to talk about their personal heroes and to point out their outstanding qualities. By the end of class, we have generated a wealth of information about heroes.

After reading these inspirational stories, the students and I embark on the yearlong journey of understanding the structure of the five-paragraph essay. To build their confidence I tell them that they are already familiar with the basics of writing an essay. All they need to do is expand what they already know about the paragraph and add to this store of knowledge. Below is the first lesson I use with my students.

Mini-Lesson 1	Comparing Paragraphs and Essays
Objective	To compare and contrast a single paragraph with the five-paragraph essay
Time	One 40-minute class period

Materials
- an overhead transparency of the paragraph titled "Qualities of a Hero" (page 20)
- four different color transparency markers
- copies of the reproducible The Paragraph and the Five-Paragraph Essay (page 21)

Step-by-Step

1. On the overhead projector show students a copy of "Qualities of a Hero." (Note that throughout the book transparencies can be created from the reproducibles supplied at the end of each chapter.)

2. Read the paragraph out loud to the class.

3. After reviewing the various parts of a paragraph, have students come up to the overhead projector and underline the topic sentence, supportive details, and clincher sentence in different colors and circle the transition words. Talk about the function of each part after students have identified it.

4. Distribute copies of The Paragraph and the Five-Paragraph Essay.

5. Read the essay in the right-hand column of the page out loud.

6. Review each paragraph of the essay and discuss the similarities and differences between the structure of the paragraph and the structure of the essay. List student responses on the board.

7. Have students work in pairs to answer the questions on the bottom of the reproducible to summarize what they have learned.

Mini-Lesson 2 | Analyzing the Structure of an Essay

The next day we quickly review the relationship between the structure of a paragraph and the structure of a five-paragraph essay. Then we microscopically analyze the makeup of the essay by engaging in the lesson below.

Objective	To analyze the structure of the five-paragraph essay
Time	One 40-minute class period
Materials	• an overhead transparency and photocopies of A Five-Paragraph Essay Model (page 23) • four different color transparency markers • four different color highlighters, markers, or pencils for each student

Step-by-Step

❶ Show the class A Five-Paragraph Essay Model on the overhead projector and hand out copies of the page to students.

❷ Explain that one of the most important parts of constructing a good essay is to understand the prompt, essay topic, or essay question. Read the prompt on A Five-Paragraph Essay Model carefully. Have students circle the key words and paraphrase the prompt. Write the paraphrase on the board and ask students to write it on their handout.

❸ Guide students through the structure of the five-paragraph essay. Examine the introduction. Through questioning and observation, lead students to see the following:

- The first sentence of the introduction should be an attention getter, the so-called hook that broadly relates to an aspect of the essay topic: heroes.

- The second and third sentences are not as broad as the first and should provide more information about the topic.

- The last sentence of the introduction is the thesis statement. The thesis expresses the main idea of the whole essay (qualities of a hero) and expresses an opinion or point of view about the topic (ordinary heroes possess universal qualities). The thesis also briefly states the topic of each body paragraph (courage, determination, and compassion).

❹ Have students highlight and label the thesis statement and number the topic of each body paragraph (1, 2, 3). Ask them to write this simple formula at the end of the introduction to help them remember how to construct the thesis:

thesis statement = main idea + opinion + three points

❺ Review each body paragraph separately and tell students to

- highlight each topic sentence. Check to be sure it relates to the appropriate point outlined in the thesis.

- number each supportive detail to be sure there are at least three.

- evaluate each supportive detail to see if it relates to the topic of the body paragraph.

- circle the transition words.

- highlight each clincher sentence. Explain that the clincher does at least one of the following: summarizes the main idea of the body paragraph or leads into the next body paragraph.

❻ Analyze the conclusion. Guide students to discover that

- the first sentence of the conclusion relates back to the introduction. Tell students to highlight and label the reference to the detail from the introduction ("Abraham Lincoln or Spider-Man").

- the thesis is explained again. Ask students to underline and label the restatement of the thesis. ("However, their courage, determination, and compassion inspire others to make changes, overcome obstacles, and reach out to those in need.")

- the main points are summarized briefly.

- a powerful closing statement appears. Have students evaluate this statement and ask them to offer equally strong alternatives.

Mini-Lesson 3 Building a Lego Model

Because research has demonstrated that "the brain learns best when it 'does' rather than 'absorbs'" (Tomlinson & Kalbfleisch, 1998), I encourage students to use Legos, Tinkertoys, or similar playthings to build a model of the five-paragraph essay. As they manipulate various building toys to design a model of a paragraph, students are "doing" rather than "absorbing" and thus increase their chances of retaining information.

Objective	To use Legos to construct a model of a five-paragraph essay To orally explain the relationship between the model and the essay
Time	One or two 40-minute class periods

Materials	• a small bag of Legos per group of four students (number each bag)
	• one of the following for each group:
	    • envelope
	    • index card
	    • pair of scissors
	    • roll of transparent tape
	    • pocket folder

Step-by-Step

1. Divide students into pairs. Then have partners take several minutes to discuss everything they can remember about a five-paragraph essay.

2. Explain to students that they will be constructing Lego models to represent the five-paragraph essay. Show them they can use different shapes and colors to symbolize the parts of an essay. Instruct students to cut apart the index card to make labels that indicate which part of the essay each segment of their model represents. Provide an example of what you expect.

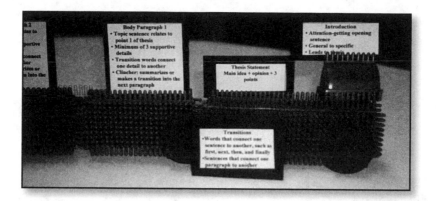

③ Have students form groups of four. Then ask them to number themselves from 1 to 4. Assign the following group roles:

#1—Labeler The labeler will

- cut the index card apart to make as many labels as the group needs for its model.
- create labels on pieces of the index card for the various parts of the five-paragraph essay.
- tape the labels to the model.

#2—Reporter The reporter will

- show the completed model to the class.
- explain how the model relates to the five-paragraph essay.

#3—Gopher The gopher will

- gather and return the materials.
- write the Lego bag number and name of each group member on the envelope.
- remove the labels from the model after it has been shown to the class and place them in the envelope.
- write the names of the group members on the front of the pocket folder.

#4—Sketcher The sketcher will

- draw a picture of the model and label its parts.

All group members will participate in building the model.

④ Write group directions on the board.

A. As a group, decide what to build as your model. (3–5 minutes)

B. Build the model. Each group member should build at least one section of it. (10–15 minutes)

C. Label the parts of the model. (3–5 minutes)

D. Draw a sketch of the model, including the labels.

⑤ After the models are built, each reporter will share his or her group's finished product with the class and explain how it relates to the five-paragraph essay.

⑥ Clean up the materials. You can store the envelopes containing the labels as well as the sketches of the models in pocket folders.

Note: If the activity takes more than one class period, set aside time the next day to have each gopher retrieve the same bag of Legos that his or her group used to build the original model. The group can then use their sketch to rebuild the model quickly. Since the appropriate labels are stored in the envelope, they can easily be taped to the model.

Teacher Tip

Instead of building a model of the five-paragraph essay, have students individually sketch an original drawing and label its parts. They can also compose a song that reviews the essay's structure. In addition, individual students may want to use play dough to sculpt their interpretation of the essay's structure.

Mini-Lesson 4 — Webbing and the Rule of Three

After students are familiar with the basic structure of the five-paragraph essay, they are ready to begin writing about the qualities of a hero. I then take the time to explain that we are all going to use the same format for prewriting—a web. It is helpful to point out that brain research shows that webs and other types of graphic organizers are powerful learning tools because they help store information in long-term memory (Sprenger, 1999). In addition, I introduce students to my Rule of Three for webbing: every branch of the web that extends from the main idea must have a cluster of three circles:

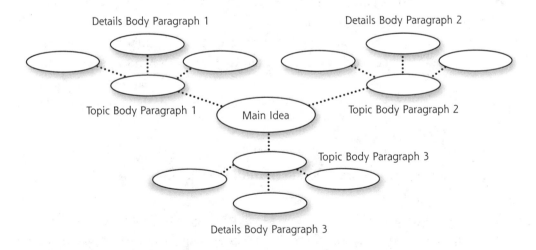

To help students better understand the concept of webbing, I use the following lesson:

Objective   To construct a prewriting web for the five-paragraph essay using the Rule of Three

Time   One 40-minute class period

Step-by-Step

① On the overhead projector, show students the Model Web for Qualities of a Hero. Distribute copies of the page to the class. Then take time to carefully explain the thinking process involved in constructing the web. Use the following script and point to the appropriate parts as you describe them:

> *In the center circle of the web is written the main idea of the prompt: Qualities of a Hero. Below that I wrote my hero's name: Grandma Jean. Inside the three circles that branch out from the main idea, I jotted down my hero's outstanding qualities: courage, determination, and compassion. Below each trait I explained why it is important. Finally, in the three circles located around each heroic quality, I listed examples of what that person does to illustrate the character trait.*

② Ask students to choose an individual who demonstrates several heroic qualities.

③ Draw a blueprint of the Rule of Three web on the board. Use colored chalk to code related clusters of circles. During the drafting process, this makes it easier for students to recognize that all circles of one color, such as the blue circles, form a single body paragraph. Once the blueprint is finished, ask students what information belongs in each circle.

④ Have students construct their own Rule of Three web on notebook paper. Insist that they color code it. Tell them to refer back to their copy of the model web if they need to.

As students draw their web, they sometimes have difficulty filling in all of the circles. Usually this problem is resolved when I ask them questions about their hero or about why the qualities they have chosen are important. While students work, I circulate around the room and check each web to be sure it is detailed enough and that the information relates to the essay topic. Otherwise, they will experience difficulty with their drafts. Because this is the first five-paragraph essay I have students write, I insist that they use the web. Later, when they have internalized the structure of the five-paragraph essay, I allow students to choose their own method of prewriting. Interestingly, most prefer webbing.

> **Technology Connection**
>
> An excellent technology tool for constructing webs is a software program called Inspiration. Without exception, my students prefer making their webs on the computer.

Mini-Lesson 5 Constructing the Thesis Statement

Once students have completed their web, show them how to use it to construct an appropriate thesis statement, utilizing the steps outlined below.

Objective   To write the thesis for the five-paragraph essay

Time	One or two 40-minute class periods
Materials	• an overhead transparency of the Model Web for Qualities of a Hero (page 25) • an overhead transparency of A Five-Paragraph Essay Model (page 23) • an overhead transparency marker • colored chalk

Step-by-Step

❶ Ask students to put their webs, pencils, and drafting paper on their desks. Then on the overhead projector show the Model Web for Qualities of a Hero.

❷ Demonstrate how to use the web to construct the thesis. To form the three-point thesis statement, have students take the topic of the essay (qualities of a hero), make their own statement about it (ordinary heroes possess universal qualities), and create the three points used to develop the body paragraphs from the circles containing the heroic qualities (courage, determination, and compassion). After explaining how to use the web to come up with a strong thesis statement, show A Five-Paragraph Essay Model on the overhead and underline the thesis statement. Remind students that the thesis statement = main idea + opinion + three points.

❸ Before students attempt to write their own thesis statement, use the information contained on several of the webs to construct a variety of model statements. Write these on the board. Underline the main idea in each one and number the three points. Ask students if the thesis contains an opinion about or attitude toward the subject of the essay. Consider using the following thinking pattern as you analyze the student-generated thesis statements:

Student thesis:	Three qualities a hero must possess are intelligence, kindness, and patience.
Main idea =	qualities of a hero
Opinion about/attitude toward subject =	A hero <u>must</u> <u>have</u> these three qualities or he/she is not a hero.
Three points =	intelligence kindness patience

Teacher Tip

If students experience difficulty constructing the thesis statement, simplify the process. Reduce the formula to main idea + three points. Later add the idea that a thesis should also express an opinion or attitude toward the essay subject.

❹ As soon as students demonstrate a basic understanding of the concept, ask them to think up their own thesis statement. When they are finished writing, have them come up to the front of the room in small groups and write their statement legibly on the board. After dividing the class into pairs, ask students to take turns using colored chalk to underline the main idea in their partner's thesis statement and number the three points. If the partner thinks the thesis expresses an opinion or attitude toward the subject, tell him or her to add a check mark in front of the statement.

❺ Provide time for you and your students to read all of the thesis statements. As you analyze each one, note any problems. Then have the class work as a group to correct these issues.

Mini-Lesson 6 | Hooking Readers With the Introduction

After students create a solid thesis statement, they are ready to draft the introduction.

Objective	To draft the introduction of the five-paragraph essay
Time	20 minutes
Materials	• an overhead transparency and photocopies of A Five-Paragraph Essay Model (page 23) • an overhead transparency marker

Step-by-Step

❶ On the overhead, point out the introduction to A Five-Paragraph Essay Model. As a review, pair up students and ask them to take turns stating the characteristics of an effective introduction: a general attention-getting sentence related to the essay topic; two or three sentences related to the essay topic that become more specific; a three-point thesis statement. Have partners identify these characteristics in the sample introduction.

❷ After students review the model, point out that introductory paragraphs use different techniques to grab the reader's attention. For example, this essay mentions two famous people, Abraham Lincoln and Spider-Man, to hook the reader. Other "hooks" include asking a question or beginning with a surprising statement, anecdote, quotation, or analogy. Instruct students to take out their thesis statement and draft the introduction. Remind them to use the thesis as the last sentence of their paragraph.

Note: The reproducible Five Approaches to Attention-Getting Introductions (page 26) provides some examples of hooks for students to peruse. Other examples appear throughout this book in the model paragraphs.

❸ When students have completed their introduction, read several sample paragraphs written by former students to the class. Together, evaluate each one based on the criteria listed under Step 1. Then pair up the class and ask partners to take turns reading their paragraph out loud, listening for the three characteristics of an effective introduction. If any are missing or if the introduction is unclear, have students suggest revisions.

To simplify the introduction for younger students or reluctant writers, have them begin with an attention-getting sentence. In their second sentence they should state the main idea of the essay. In the third sentence they need to come up with the topic for body paragraph one. The fourth and fifth sentences should then spell out the topics for body paragraphs two and three, respectively.

Mini-Lesson 7 Drafting the Body Paragraphs

Objective	To construct the three body paragraphs of the five-paragraph essay
Time	One or two 40-minute class periods
Materials	• an overhead transparency of the Model Web for Qualities of a Hero (page 25) • an overhead transparency of A Five-Paragraph Essay Model (page 23) • four different color transparency markers (e.g., red, green, blue, purple)

Step-by-Step

❶ Ask students to put aside their webs and introductions. Then, on the overhead, project the Model Web for Qualities of a Hero.

❷ Demonstrate to the class how to use the web to form each body paragraph of their essay. Have students look at the cluster of circles containing the topic of the first body paragraph (courage) and the three details used to illustrate this idea. Show them that the heroic quality courage becomes the main idea of the topic sentence for the paragraph. The three circles branching out from *courage* then become the supportive details.

❸ Next, display the first body paragraph of the essay model on the overhead projector to solidify its connection with the web. Underline the topic sentence in red. Circle the word *courage*. Then remind the class that the topic sentence explains why courage is important because the essay prompt states this must be done. Also examine the thesis statement. Courage is the first of the three points. Therefore, it must be the topic of the first body paragraph. In green number each supportive detail. Discuss each detail's relationship to the web. Remind students that they should write at least one sentence about each relevant circle on the web to create three supportive details in the body paragraph. Circle transition words in purple and talk about the need to connect one idea to another. Underline the clincher sentence in blue. Review the possible functions of the clincher: It summarizes the main idea of the body paragraph, leads into the next paragraph, or does both.

❹ Provide time for students to draft their first body paragraph. Then write the directions below on the board and instruct partners to exchange drafts and perform the following steps:

Underline the topic sentence. Circle the heroic quality. Draw a box around the reason why this character trait is important.

Number the supportive details.

Circle the transition words.

Underline the clincher.

If anything is missing or does not make sense, tell the writer and together make your revisions.

⑤ Repeat steps 2–4, instructing the class to draft body paragraphs two and three. Encourage students to work with different partners each time they peer edit a new paragraph so they can review different writing styles and receive feedback from more than one person.

Mini-Lesson 8   Coming Up With the Conclusion

Objective	To write the conclusion of the five-paragraph essay
Time	20 minutes
Materials	• an overhead transparency of A Five-Paragraph Essay Model (page 23) • an overhead transparency marker

Step-by-Step

① On the overhead projector display the conclusion of A Five-Paragraph Essay Model.

② Read the conclusion out loud and review the essential characteristics of the final paragraph of the essay: includes a detail from the introduction that wraps up the essay; restates the thesis in a new, compelling way; summarizes the major points; and ends with a powerful image or statement. Then pair up students and have them identify these characteristics in the model.

③ Instruct students to draft their own conclusions.

④ When they finish writing, ask volunteers to share their work. As a class, evaluate each conclusion based on the criteria listed under Step 2. Then instruct partners to read their paragraph out loud to one another and listen for the four characteristics of an effective conclusion. If any are missing or if the conclusion is unclear, have students suggest revisions.

> To simplify the conclusion for younger students, have them restate the main idea of the essay in a new way in their first sentence. In the second, third, and fourth sentences have them summarize the main idea of each body paragraph. The fifth sentence should end the essay with a powerful punch.

Revising, Proofreading, and Assessing

Throughout the process of writing the five-paragraph essay, students have already engaged in peer editing and have provided suggestions for revision. Before they write their final copies, have them form small proofreading groups and assign the following roles:

Spell Checker—circles misspelled words and labels them (**sp**).

Sentence Monitor—brackets and labels run-ons, fragments, and sentences that do not make sense. **[ ] R.O.   [ ] Frag.   [ ] S.S.**

Mechanics Person—uses proofreading symbols to show the writer where to correct capitalization and punctuation.

As the essay drafts are passed from one group member to another, each person proofreads the paper, checking only the element he or she has have been assigned. If you choose to have students take a final look at the organization of the essay, ask partners to exchange papers and use the reproducible General Editing Checklist for the Five-Paragraph Essay (page 27) to review their work. Instruct the class to use the following symbols to fill in the blanks on the checklist:

✓ = **everything is included**

✓– = **needs work**

0 = **not there**

I always hand out a copy of the General Editing Checklist for students to keep in their notebooks. Each time we write an essay, I encourage them take out the list and review it carefully.

Assessment

To assess each student's completed paper, I use the Rubric for a Five-Paragraph Essay (page 28), an analytic guide based on the criteria defined by the Pennsylvania Department of Education: focus, organization, content, usage, and style. I like this rubric because it is generic enough to use with most five-paragraph essays.

Although the steps involved in introducing a thoughtful, well-constructed essay are time-consuming, the end product is worth the effort. The process outlined here is the most effective one I have used to date; quite simply, it has improved the quality and content of my students' essay writing. I believe the process works well because of the strategies employed. Modeling, repetition, practice, peer interaction, graphic organizers, and color coding are all supported by current brain research (Jensen, 1998; Sprenger, 1999).

Have students bring in photographs or draw pictures of the heroes referred to in their essays. Create a bulletin board display or a *Student Heroes* book. Read a few of the essays out loud on Back-to-School Night.

Qualities of a Hero

While ordinary heroes like my Grandma Jean
are not as famous as Abraham Lincoln or Spider-Man,
they possess universal qualities, such as courage,
determination, and compassion. Courage, which is
undoubtedly a trait that most heroes display, motivates
people to make positive changes in the world. Another
heroic quality is determination, which enables individuals
to overcome challenges and difficult situations. But
perhaps the most important quality is compassion,
because caring about others and assisting those in need
make the world a more humane place to live. In
conclusion, because of their courage, determination,
and compassion, heroes inspire others to make changes,
overcome obstacles, and reach out to those in need.

The Paragraph and the Five-Paragraph Essay

The Paragraph

Topic Sentence

While ordinary **heroes** like my Grandma Jean are not as famous as Abraham Lincoln or Spider-Man, they **possess universal qualities**, such as **courage**, **determination**, and **compassion**.

Like the topic sentence of a single paragraph, the introduction of the five-paragraph essay introduces the reader to the topic. The last sentence of the introduction is the thesis statement, which states the main idea of the essay and briefly outlines the topics of the body paragraphs.

Supportive Detail One

Courage, which is undoubtedly a trait that heroes display, motivates people to make positive changes in the world.

Both supportive detail one and body paragraph one support and develop the first point in the topic sentence and thesis statement, respectively.

Supportive Detail Two

Another heroic quality is **determination**, which enables many people to overcome challenges and difficult situations.

Supportive detail two and body paragraph two support and develop the second point in the topic sentence and thesis statement, respectively.

The Five-Paragraph Essay

Introduction

Abraham Lincoln and Spider-Man are not the only heroes in the world. Heroes can be ordinary people like you and me. They can be as young as a child or as old as a senior citizen. However, as different as they might be, ordinary **heroes** like my Grandma Jean **possess universal qualities**, such as **courage**, **determination**, and **compassion**.

Body Paragraph One

Courage, which is undoubtedly a trait that heroes display, motivates people to make positive changes in the world. In a society that believed a woman's place was in the home, my grandmother's inner strength and courage allowed her to break the mold. During the 1930s she worked on Wall Street as the art editor for *Good Housekeeping* magazine, and later in her life she became the country's first Cattlewoman of the Year. Even though she was frequently the only woman in a room filled with hundreds of men, Grandma Jean still had the courage to gracefully stride up to the podium to speak about the new genetic techniques that she designed to help ordinary cattlemen improve the quality of their herds. In short, her inner strength and **courage** allowed her to serve as an advocate for women's rights.

Body Paragraph Two

Another heroic quality is **determination**, which enables many people to overcome challenges and difficult situations. Determined to help my invalid, wheelchair-bound grandfather live a normal life, my grandmother invented a creative way for him to roam the cattle pastures. Grandma Jean actually bought and renovated a Checker taxicab! Every afternoon she maneuvered my grandfather's lift and drove him from one field to another in his comfortable, king-size automobile. Without my grandmother's **determination** and creativity, my grandfather would have been trapped inside the house in his wheelchair, unable to view his beloved land and livestock.

The Paragraph and the Five-Paragraph Essay

The Paragraph

The Five-Paragraph Essay

Supportive Detail Three

But perhaps the most important quality is **compassion**, because caring about others and helping those in need make the world a more humane place to live.

Supportive detail three and body paragraph three support and develop the third point in the topic sentence and thesis statement, respectively.

Body Paragraph Three

Although courage and determination are heroic traits, perhaps the most important quality is **compassion**. Without a doubt, caring about others and helping those in need make the world a more humane place to live. For 15 years, my grandmother tirelessly and selflessly cared for my grandfather. Because he literally had no muscles, Grandma Jean awoke every hour on the hour each night to turn my grandfather on his side or back so that he would not get bedsores. When Pop-Pop's hands and arms no longer worked, my grandmother fed him, shaved him, and combed his hair. Even in the face of her own devastating battle with cancer, my grandmother continued to \show deep **compassion** by comforting and reaching out to my grandfather, other cancer patients, and her own family.

Clincher or Concluding Sentence

In conclusion, because of their **courage**, **determination**, and **compassion**, heroes inspire others to make changes, overcome obstacles, and reach out to those in need.

The clincher sentence of the paragraph and the conclusion of the essay both summarize the main idea and restate the major points in a new way.

Conclusion

Heroes like my grandmother are not as extraordinary as Abraham Lincoln or Spider-Man. However, their **courage**, **determination**, and **compassion** inspire others to make changes, overcome obstacles, and reach out to those in need. Heroes are our beacons, our guides, the people who individually and collectively promote peace, justice, love, and understanding. Because of them, our world is a better, richer place to live.

What other similarities do you see between the structure of the paragraph and the structure of the five-paragraph essay?

_____

_____

_____

What differences do you see between the two?

_____

_____

_____

A Five-Paragraph Essay Model

The Prompt

Heroes are a valuable part of our world and everyone's daily life. Identify qualities or traits heroes possess and provide examples of these qualities.

Explain why these qualities are important.

Qualities of an Extraordinarily Ordinary Hero

The introduction begins with an attention-getting sentence and moves from general statements about the topic to the specific. Finally, it ends with a three-point thesis statement that states the main idea of the essay and briefly outlines the topics of the body paragraphs.

Abraham Lincoln and Spider-Man are not the only heroes in the world. Heroes can be ordinary people like you and me. They can be as young as a child or as old as a senior citizen. However, as different as they might be, ordinary **heroes** like my Grandma Jean **possess universal qualities**, such as **courage**, **determination**, and **compassion**.

Courage, which is undoubtedly a trait that most heroes possess, motivates people to make positive changes in the world. In a society that believed a woman's place was in the home, my grandmother's inner strength and courage allowed her to break the mold. During the 1930s she worked on Wall Street as the art editor for *Good Housekeeping* magazine, and later in her life she became the country's first Cattlewoman of the Year. Even though she was frequently the only woman in a room filled with hundreds of men, Grandma Jean still had the courage to gracefully stride up to the podium to speak about the new genetic techniques that she designed to help ordinary cattlemen improve the quality of their herds. **In short**, her inner strength and **courage** allowed her to serve as an advocate for women's rights.

The topic sentence of the body paragraph relates back to the first point of the thesis. It describes a heroic quality and explains its importance. The writer then uses three specific details and examples to illustrate the heroic quality of courage. The clincher sentence begins with a transition word and summarizes the main idea.

The writer uses a transition word, "another," to introduce the second quality a hero possesses. The topic sentence relates back to the second point of the thesis. Again, three detail sentences illustrate the heroic quality. A concluding sentence summarizes the main idea.

Another admirable quality that heroes possess is **determination**, which enables many people to overcome challenges and difficult situations. Determined to help my invalid, wheelchair-bound grandfather live a normal life, my grandmother invented a creative way for him to roam the cattle pastures. Grandma Jean actually bought and renovated a Checker taxicab! Every afternoon she maneuvered my grandfather's lift and drove him from one field to another in his comfortable, king-size automobile. Without my grandmother's **determination** and creativity, my grandfather would have been trapped inside the house in his wheelchair unable to view his beloved land and livestock.

Although courage and determination are heroic traits, perhaps the most important quality is **compassion**. Without a doubt, caring about others and helping those in need make the world a more humane place to live. For 15 years my grandmother tirelessly and selflessly cared for my grandfather. Because he literally had no muscles, Grandma Jean awoke every hour on the hour each night to turn my grandfather on his side or back so that he would not get bedsores. When Pop-Pop's hands and arms no longer worked, my grandmother fed him, shaved him, and combed his hair. Even in the face of her own devastating battle with cancer, my grandmother continued to show deep **compassion** by comforting and reaching out to my grandfather, other cancer patients, and her own family.

The topic sentence of the third paragraph relates to the third point of the thesis and connects back to body paragraphs one and two. It also has three detail sentences and a clincher. Also, the writer organizes the information in the body from least important to most important.

The conclusion includes a detail from the introduction to wrap up the essay. It restates or echoes the thesis statement, summarizes the main points, and ends with a powerful statement.

Heroes like my grandmother are not as extraordinary as Abraham Lincoln or Spider-Man. However, their **courage**, **determination**, and **compassion** inspire others to make changes, overcome obstacles, and reach out to those in need. Heroes are our beacons, our guides, the people who individually and collectively promote peace, justice, love, and understanding. Because of them, our world is a better, richer place to live.

Model Web for Qualities of a Hero

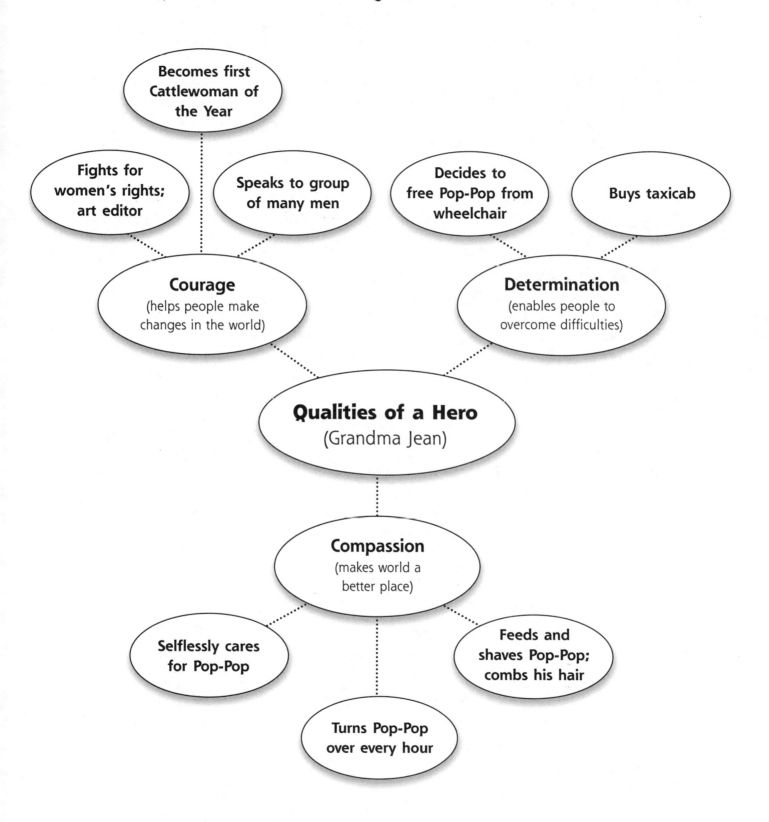

Becomes first Cattlewoman of the Year

Fights for women's rights; art editor

Speaks to group of many men

Decides to free Pop-Pop from wheelchair

Buys taxicab

Courage
(helps people make changes in the world)

Determination
(enables people to overcome difficulties)

Qualities of a Hero
(Grandma Jean)

Compassion
(makes world a better place)

Selflessly cares for Pop-Pop

Feeds and shaves Pop-Pop; combs his hair

Turns Pop-Pop over every hour

Five Approaches to Attention-Getting Introductions

To grab the reader's attention in the introduction of the five-paragraph essay, try some of the following techniques:

1 Start with an analogy.

Pounding. Forever pounding upon the anvil is the hammer. The clash of steel and iron as they meet on the cold, rusty anvil permeates the air and echoes through it. All the while, the sturdy, resilient anvil provides the support needed to withstand the blows of the hammer. It is forever the broad base to be bashed and smashed to make the iron stronger and to give the hammer strength in return. In *Great Expectations* by Charles Dickens the lower class of nineteenth-century England is the anvil; the upper class is the hammer. Through his portrait of the social classes, Dickens illustrates that social rank causes people to act foolishly, misjudge character, and lose themselves in order to conform to society's expectations.   *—Cassidy Quilty*

2 Ask a question.

How many times have you been told to remove your lazy derriere from the computer and exercise instead? The truth is computers are a huge part of everybody's life. From business offices to your own living room, computers are everywhere. In contemporary society, people must be computer literate to survive. Used to type documents, access the Internet, and communicate, the computer has become a necessity in today's new world. *—Stephanie Povirk*

3 Use a quotation.

"To err is human, to forgive is divine." Alexander Pope's words are relevant in contemporary society and in *Great Expectations* by Charles Dickens. In both worlds, the collective society forgets that all humans make mistakes and deserve forgiveness. Dickens echoes this theme by openly mocking society for its inability to forgive Magwitch for his crimes and to allow him once again to live a new life. Throughout the course of the novel Pip, the protagonist, learns about man's inhumanity to man. He discovers that many innocent people are punished unfairly, that many horrible people are considered to be respectable, and that jails do not denote the inner worth of a person.   *—Cole Pierce*

4 Begin with an enticing sensory description of the setting.

Freshly cut grass. Blooming tulips. Warming temperatures. Springtime had arrived. Our lunchtime chatter remained the same, brimming with gossip of boys, classes, and get-togethers. But on that fateful morning, our lunch table buzzed with the excitement of the upcoming softball season.   *—Cassie Leighton*

5 Create an interesting simile.

Growth without experience is like a bridge without support. In *Great Expectations* by Charles Dickens, the protagonist Pip struggles to bridge the gap between the lower and upper classes as he strives to attain higher social status. Dickens illustrates that true growth can only happen in stages. Thus, as Pip's expectations shatter, he discovers his internal weaknesses, removes his blinders, and becomes a true gentleman.   *—Mark Rossborough*

Name _____ Date _____ Section _____

General Editing Checklist for the Five-Paragraph Essay

| ✓ = everything is included | ✓– = needs work | 0 = not there |

The Introduction

_____ Begins with an attention-getting sentence related to the essay topic.

_____ Moves from general information about the topic to more specific information.

_____ Contains a three-point thesis statement that clearly states the main idea of the essay, expresses an opinion or point of view about the topic, and briefly outlines the subject of each body paragraph.

_____ Is three to five sentences in length.

The Body

_____ Has a topic sentence that relates back to the thesis.

_____ Develops its topic and supports it with a minimum of three specific details.

_____ Contains two or three transition words or phrases that connect one idea to another.

_____ Contains a clincher or concluding sentence. This sentence summarizes the main idea of the paragraph, leads into the next paragraph, or does both.

_____ Transitions between body paragraphs are evident and clear. One paragraph flows naturally into another.

_____ The paragraphs are clear, logical, and easy to understand.

The Conclusion

_____ Includes a detail or example from the introduction that wraps up the essay.

_____ Restates, or echoes, the thesis statement without simply repeating it.

_____ Summarizes the major points.

_____ Ends with a strong image or powerful statement.

_____ Is three to five sentences in length.

Rubric for a Five-Paragraph Essay

	4	3	2	1
Focus 4 3 2 1	Consistently establishes and maintains a clear purpose and point of view related to the audience and task	Generally establishes and maintains a clear purpose and point of view related to the audience and task	Has some difficulty establishing and maintaining a clear purpose and point of view related to the audience and task	Does not clearly establish or maintain a purpose and/or point of view related to the audience and task
Organization 4 3 2 1	Highly effective introduction containing a 3-point thesis; 3 body paragraphs related to thesis that include logical transitions within and between paragraphs; a comprehensive conclusion that powerfully summarizes the main points	Effective introduction containing a 3-point thesis; 3 body paragraphs related to thesis that include logical transitions within and between paragraphs; a comprehensive conclusion that powerfully summarizes the main points	Moderately effective introduction containing a thesis; 3 body paragraphs somewhat related to thesis that include some logical transitions within and between paragraphs; a conclusion that summarizes the main points	Ineffective introduction, body, and conclusion; weak thesis or no thesis; little evidence of transitions within and between paragraphs
Content 4 3 2 1	Thorough development of ideas and details that are related to the topic	Substantial development of ideas and details that are related to the topic	Partial development of ideas and details that are related to the topic	Incomplete development of ideas and details that are related to the topic
Usage (Conventions) 4 3 2 1	Accurate use of mechanics, spelling, grammar, and sentence structure	Generally accurate use of mechanics, spelling, grammar, and sentence structure	Somewhat accurate use of mechanics, spelling, grammar, and sentence structure	Major inaccuracies in the use of mechanics, spelling, grammar, and sentence structure
Style 4 3 2 1	Highly effective use of precise language, word choice, voice, and sentence variety	Effective use of precise language, word choice, voice, and sentence variety	Moderately effective use of precise language, word choice, voice, and sentence variety	Ineffective use of precise language, word choice, voice, and sentence variety

*T*he Informational Essay

Background Information

*J*ust as its name suggests, the purpose of informational writing is to provide knowledge or facts about a particular subject or topic. For example, informational writing may be used to explain a process, give directions, or tell why something happens. In addition, it can be used to define, classify, summarize, compare, contrast, or demonstrate cause-and-effect relationships. Because of the broad function and extensive use of informational writing both in schools and in the workplace, it is important to provide students with multiple opportunities to engage in this type of essay writing.

Although most informational essays are factual, follow a specific format, and are written in the third person, they need not be boring. This is one of the reasons why I choose to use "Cell Phone Mania" (page 38) to introduce my students to the informational essay. Not only does it follow the prescribed format, but it also shows students how to incorporate voice and style into their writing. In addition, I am a firm believer in raising the bar: If you provide students with a model that goes beyond the minimum requirements, they will produce better writing.

Getting Started

After we finish reading *Travels With Charley* by John Steinbeck, I present the prompt and mini-lesson on page 30.

Informational Prompt:
How Technology Affects Society

In *Travels With Charley*, John Steinbeck observes not only his own interest in new "gadgets," but also society's infatuation with anything different and innovative. He writes:

Civilization had made great strides in my absence. I remember when a coin in a slot would get you a stick of gum or a candy bar, but in these dining places were vending machines where various coins could deliver handkerchiefs, comb-and-nail-file sets, hair conditioners and cosmetics, first-aid kits, and minor drugs such as aspirin, mild physics, pills to keep you awake. I found myself entranced with these gadgets. (p. 90)

As Steinbeck notes, gadgets have a powerful effect on him as well as on "civilization." Similarly, today's technological "gadgets," such as cell phones, laptops, and palm pilots, have a dramatic impact on society. Technology has certainly transformed the way we live our lives.

Choose a technological device and explain how this new technology affects society.

 **Mini-Lesson 1**

Reading and Responding to an Informational Prompt

Objective	To define informational writing and provide the class with examples To read and interpret an informational prompt To use the Rule of Three to generate a class web for the prompt
Time	One 40-minute class period
Materials	• an overhead transparency or photocopies of the informational prompt (see above)

Step-by-Step

1 Write the phrase *informational essay* on the board. Challenge students to define this type of writing as well as to provide two or three examples from any books they are currently reading.

2 Either distribute copies of the prompt to students or show an overhead transparency to the class.

3 Read and examine the prompt carefully. Circle the key words (*choose, technological device, explain how, technology, affects, society*).

4 Instruct students to state the topic and purpose of the prompt. Through questioning, guide them to the following:

> Topic: Effects of technology on society
>
> Purpose: To explain how a technological device affects society

5 Tell students to brainstorm individually a list of technological inventions that affect their lives in some way. Ask them to share their ideas and take turns writing their suggestions on the board. Then have students agree on the one technological device they will use as an essay topic.

6 Ask students to generate ideas about how to develop their topic. Refer them back to the prompt, the topic, and its purpose. Lead students to understand that the major pattern of organization for their essay will be to discuss the *effects* of their technological device on life today. Note that although Steinbeck believes "gadgets" have a positive influence on society, these items may have a negative impact as well. Tell students to consider both the positive and negative effects of technology as they develop their webs.

7 On the board, draw a color-coded partial blueprint of the Rule of Three web (see Mini-Lesson 4, page 12).

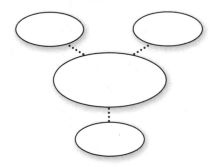

8 Ask the class what to write in the main idea circle of the web (*Effect of Technology on Society*). Jot this down on the board. After students have agreed on a specific technological device, write the name of the invention above the word *Technology*. Then challenge the class to think of three major effects this technological tool has had on our everyday lives. Write these inside the three circles branching out from the main idea. Remind students of the Rule of Three: Each effect must be explained and supported by three examples or facts. Finish constructing the class web. Follow the procedure outlined in Mini-Lesson 4 on page 13.

9 Tell students to construct their own color-coded web on notebook paper.

| | Mini-Lesson 2 | # Modeling the Informational Essay |

Objective
To model a five-paragraph informational essay
To review the structure of a five-paragraph essay
To generate thesis statements for an informational essay

Time
One 40-minute class period

Materials
- an overhead transparency and photocopies of Web 2: Effect of Technology on Society (page 37)
- an overhead transparency and photocopies of "Cell Phone Mania" (page 38)

Step-by-Step

① Distribute copies of Web 2: Effects of Technology on Society and display a copy of it from the overhead projector. Have students carefully read and examine the web.

② In groups of three or four, have students generate a thesis statement based on the web. Ask the following questions to help them get started: *What is the formula for a thesis statement?* (Have a student write this on the board: main idea + opinion + three points.) *What is the main idea of this essay? What is the author's opinion of the effect of the cell phone on society? What three points should be included in the thesis statement?*

③ Instruct one person from each group to write their thesis statement on the board, underline the main idea, and number the three points. As a class, evaluate the thesis statements.

④ Hand out copies of "Cell Phone Mania" to students, and project a copy of it from the overhead projector. Read the whole essay out loud to the class.

⑤ Use the model to review the structure of the five-paragraph essay (see Mini-Lesson 2 on page 8 as well as the comments in the margins of "Cell Phone Mania"). Ask questions about the structure to elicit this information from the class. When examining the introduction, compare and contrast each group's thesis statement to the one supplied by the author.

⑥ Through questioning, emphasize the following:

- The introduction begins with an intriguing question.

- Sometimes extra sentences are added to the body paragraphs for further elaboration.

- Transition words within paragraphs are critical in order to connect one sentence to another. (Ask students to find and circle all of the transition words within the body paragraphs.)

- Transition sentences can be used to connect one paragraph to another.
- The writer
  - organizes the essay by elaborating on the effects of cell phones on society and includes examples of these effects.

  - does not use the pronoun *I* in the essay. (Explain that most informational essays try to avoid using the pronoun *you* as well. However, in this particular case *you* works because it draws the reader into the essay and is part of the writer's style.)

  - uses humor and questions to express her opinion about the topic. (Have students find examples of this and define *style*.)

  - has a strong voice. (Have students identify sentences that reveal the author's voice. Ask them to describe and cite examples of the author's style.)

Students are now ready to draft their essays. Because the process of writing a five-paragraph essay is still relatively new and has not yet been internalized, I assign one paragraph of the essay per night for homework. The following day we peer edit and revise each paragraph in a manner similar to the one described in activities 5–8 (pages 13–19). For this essay, I instruct students to write their thesis statement on the board for partner and class evaluation because this is the most difficult part of the assignment for them to master. Also, if a student begins with a weak thesis statement, the whole essay is likely to fall apart.

Variation of Mini-Lesson 2

For younger students and reluctant writers, you may want to use a slightly different method for writing a five-paragraph informational essay. The basic format is the same as the one above; however, the essay itself is more formal and the guidelines more prescriptive. "The Amazing Internet" (page 40) follows this pattern. It is a shortened version of an essay written by my student Casey. Below is an outline of the format he used to construct it. To incite a lively discussion about five-paragraph essays in your class, have students debate which of the two informational pieces is better and why. To differentiate instruction, model both essays and allow students to choose the approach that best fits their particular learning style.

Paragraph 1: Introduction

    A. Attention-getting topic sentence

    B. Sentence about topic of body paragraph one (subtopic one)

    C. Sentence about topic of body paragraph two (subtopic two)

    D. Sentence about topic of body paragraph three (subtopic three)

    E. Thesis statement (main idea/topic + writer's opinion about the topic)

Paragraph 2: First Body Paragraph

    A. Restatement of subtopic sentence one from the introduction

    B. First supportive detail or example

    C. Second supportive detail or example

    D. Third supportive detail or example

    E. Clincher sentence/transition into the next body paragraph

Paragraph 3: Second Body Paragraph

    A. Restatement of subtopic sentence two from the introduction

    B. First supportive detail or example

    C. Second supportive detail or example

    D. Third supportive detail or example

    E. Clincher sentence/transition into the next body paragraph

Paragraph 4: Third Body Paragraph

    A. Restatement of subtopic sentence three from the introduction

    B. First supportive detail or example

    C. Second supportive detail or example

    D. Third supportive detail or example

    E. Clincher sentence/transition into the conclusion

Paragraph 5: Conclusion

    A. Restatement of thesis

    B. Summary of subtopic one

    C. Summary of subtopic two

    D. Summary of subtopic three

    E. Concluding sentence

The Missing Link: An Activity to Teach Transition Words

The reproducible titled The Missing Link (page 41) is a student example of an informational essay on the effect of technology on society. The sample includes the first three of the five paragraphs. All of the transition words have been omitted. Use some of the ideas listed on page 36 with your students.

Divide students into groups of four. Then distribute copies of the reproducible pages A List of Transitions (page 42) and The Missing Link (page 41). Have the groups work together to fill in all of the missing words. If they need any help, tell students to refer to the list of transition words. The group that finishes first and has correct responses (ones that make sense) earns a roll of Smarties or another appropriate prize. Compare and contrast all of the answers supplied by each group.

Possible answers for The Missing Link: 1. Yet 2. First 3. When 4. also 5. Finally 6. In brief 7. Second 8. For example 9. Another 10. In addition 11. Consequently

Variation

Enlarge the reproducible to poster size, and laminate it. When hung on the wall, it will serve as a useful learning center. Have students take an overhead marker to fill in all of the blanks. Provide an answer key. Or use card stock to make transition word cards approximately the same size as the blanks. After cutting out and laminating each one, place Velcro on the back of the card as well as on the poster blanks. Then challenge students to attach the appropriate word cards to the poster.

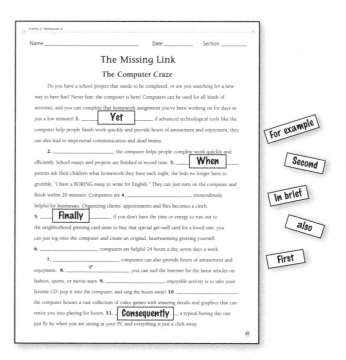

Other Activities for Teaching Transition Words

- Collect examples of sentences written by a previous class that either use the wrong transition word or have no transition word at all. Then write the sentences on an overhead transparency and challenge students to make any needed changes.

- Have students compare and contrast an essay from another class that effectively uses transition words and one that either omits them or uses them incorrectly. In pairs, groups, or as a class, revise the essay with problems.

- Create a handout with four or five different types of paragraphs, including ones that use sequence or chronological order, that compare and contrast various items, that describe a person or place, and that show cause-and-effect relationships. Omit the transitions and challenge the class to generate the missing words.

- Type out a completed essay written by a former student. Omit all the clincher sentences as well as the topic sentences of the three body paragraphs. Then have groups of students collaborate to write transition sentences that effectively connect one paragraph to another.

- Have students cut apart the five paragraphs of their draft, mix them up, and give them to a partner, whose job is to then rearrange the paragraphs in the correct order. If any transition words are missing and the student has problems reorganizing the essay, initiate a discussion about which transitions work effectively and which ones do not. As a result, direct the writer to change or add transitions to the paper. In addition to focusing on how one paragraph flows smoothly into another, partners should circle the transition words within the paragraphs as well and evaluate their effectiveness.

Note: This activity is derived from a presentation titled "The Art of Revision: Puzzling Paragraphs—A Kinesthetic Activity for Revision and Editing" by Ellie Stewart and is used with permission.

Web 2: Effect of Technology on Society

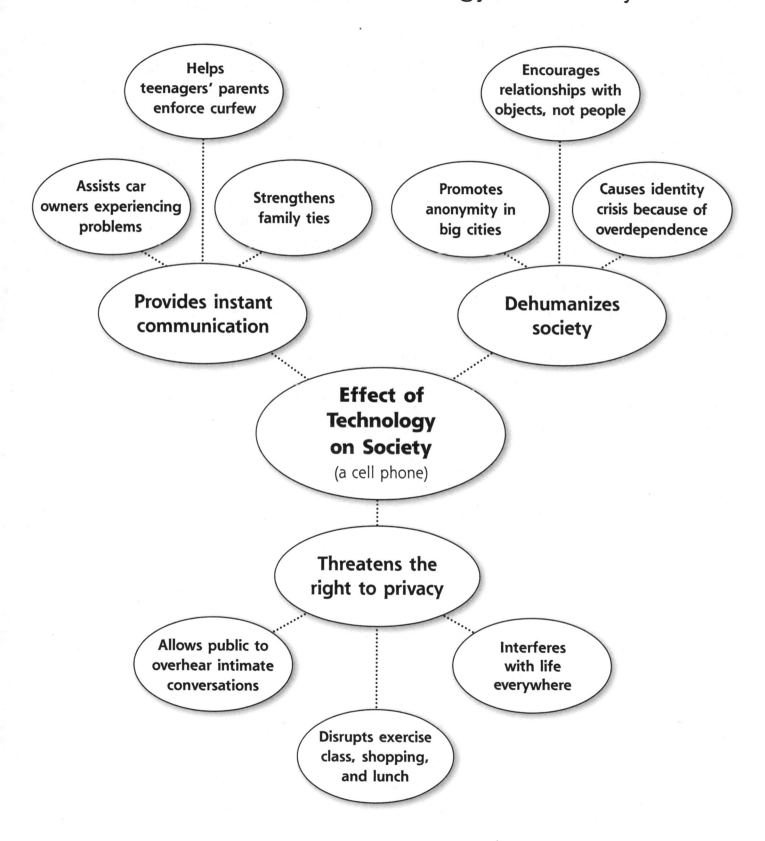

Informational Essay Model 1

Cell Phone Mania

The introduction begins with an interesting question to grab the reader's attention. It concludes with a thesis statement that states the topic of the essay and the writer's opinion about the topic. It also outlines each of the body paragraphs.

Did your grandmother's 1980 Chevy just blow two rear tires on a rural dirt road in the Blue Ridge Mountains? Don't worry; pick up your cell phone and dial 1-800-AAA-Auto. Whether you are stuck in a horrendous traffic jam or relaxing in a romantic restaurant, one of the world's latest high-tech gadgets, the cell phone, may be either the answer to your prayers or a major pain in your derriere. Like it or not, the cell phone is here to stay. While this technological device positively affects society by **providing instant communication**, it also **dehumanizes relationships** and **threatens an individual's right to privacy**.

One positive effect of the cell phone on American society is its ability to **provide instant communication**. **First**, the device is invaluable to car owners who possess vehicles that won't budge an inch. Nothing makes a motorist with a defective starter or a faulty transmission happier than dialing AAA on his or her cell phone and listening to the manager say, "The tow truck should arrive in ten minutes." **Second**, cell phones help keep parents and their children in touch. For example, at a minute before midnight the parents of a 16-year-old can call their son's cell phone and gently shriek, "If you are not home within ten minutes, you will be grounded for the next six months." **Third**, if a loved one is in the service and is stationed somewhere around the world, family members can pick up the cell phone and report that Susie took her first step or that Johnny lost his front tooth. **In short**, the cell phone's ability to allow anyone to be reached at any time soothes America's collective psyche.

The topic sentence relates back to the thesis and is supported by three details. Sometimes extra sentences are added to further explain a detail. Transition words, such as first, second, and third, connect one idea to another.

A clincher sentence summarizes the information.

Mastering the Five-Paragraph Essay Scholastic Teaching Resources

Here the topic sentence makes a transition from the first body paragraph into the second. The topic sentence is directly derived from the thesis.

Ironically, **the technological device that binds society together also threatens to destroy it through the process of dehumanization**. Just stride down Lexington Avenue in New York City and in less than five minutes you will observe a hundred men, women, and yes, even children ignoring each other as they blather mindlessly into their cell phones. Literally, cell phones are replacing living, breathing human beings. Some phone owners, for example, can be heard whispering sweet nothings to their beloved cells, such as "Where are you, Snookieookums?" Recently, one moviegoer experienced an identity crisis when she lost her phone. Before fainting, she mournfully cried, "Where is my phone, my right hand?" All in all, the cell phone, along with other technological advancements, removes the "human" element from society.

Finally, the cell phone **threatens an individual's right to privacy**. How many intimate conversations between lawyers and clients, doctors and patients, or husbands and wives have you unwittingly overheard this week? How many times has your exercise class, shopping spree, or lunch been abruptly disrupted by the annoying sound of *Take Me Out to the Ballgame* playing in someone's pocket or purse? No conversation and no location are too sacred for the cell phone. At the rate cell phone use is expanding, the word *privacy* will soon disappear from our vocabulary.

The topic sentence of the third body paragraph is also derived from the thesis statement.

Notice that the writer's anger is conveyed through questions. The style enhances the paper's tone and voice.

The conclusion refers back to the "romantic restaurant" used in the introduction. In addition, it summarizes the main idea, refers back to the thesis statement, and ends with a powerful punch.

So, your beau tried to pop the big question at Chez Mystique but you couldn't hear him, because another diner's cell phone conversation drowned out his soft, romantic words. Why just yesterday when you were hopelessly lost in Boston, you kissed your cell after calling a friend for directions! Even though cell phones, the great communicators, dehumanize relationships and threaten our privacy, they are too deeply embedded in today's society to become obsolete.

Informational Essay Model 2

The Amazing Internet

The Internet is one of the most influential technological devices ever created. First, the "Net" improves communication between friends, relatives, and coworkers. Second, it makes research substantially easier. Third, this technology tool promotes laziness. Why go from store to store or from library to library when you can just as easily surf the Net? Without a doubt, the Internet has both positive and negative effects on modern society as we know it today.

First of all, the Internet makes communication between friends and family easier. For example, instead of writing a letter, news can be sent via e-mail. Furthermore, e-mail is sent and received instantly, so the person on the receiving end does not have to wait several days for a letter. Moreover, unlike the telephone, instant messaging on the Internet allows friends to have multiple conversations simultaneously. To summarize, the Internet provides faster, easier, more reliable communication.

A second positive effect of the Internet is that it simplifies the research process. As any student will tell you, the Net virtually eliminates the need for actual books, magazines, and newspapers. Using the Net is also more efficient than traipsing to the local library. It connects the researcher instantly to multiple links and sources. In addition, the Internet speeds up the research process because clicking several computer keys takes much less time than locating a book. All in all, the Internet has made completing research projects easier and less time-consuming. Yet, despite all these advantages, use of the Net has also created a number of real problems.

One negative effect of the Internet is that it encourages laziness. Instead of writing long letters with beautiful handwriting, people send quick e-mails filled with misspellings and grammatical mistakes. Second, even though books often contain more reliable information than Internet sources, they frequently are not used because the Net offers easy access to a huge range of facts, figures, and stunning graphics. Furthermore, the Internet's game, music, and sport sites are so entertaining that millions of people view them for hours, forget to exercise, and are at risk for becoming obese. In conclusion, the technology tool that improves lives also has some real disadvantages.

The Internet, a valuable invention, has both beneficial and harmful effects on society. It allows friends and relatives to communicate quickly and frequently. It also makes doing research much, much easier. On the other hand, the Internet causes people to sit in the same place, hour after hour, glued to their computer screens, which is clearly not a healthy thing. In sum, even though the Net promotes laziness, it is still one of the world's greatest technological innovations.

Name _____   Date _____   Section _____

The Missing Link

The Computer Craze

Do you have a school project that needs to be completed, or are you searching for a new way to have fun? Never fear; the computer is here! Computers can be used for all kinds of activities, and you can complete that homework assignment you've been working on for days in just a few minutes! **1.** _____, if advanced technological tools like the computer help people finish work quickly and provide hours of amusement and enjoyment, they can also lead to impersonal communication and dead brains.

2. _____, the computer helps people complete work quickly and efficiently. School essays and projects are finished in record time. **3.** _____ parents ask their children what homework they have each night, the kids no longer have to grumble, "I have a BORING essay to write for English." They can just turn on the computer and finish within 20 minutes. Computers are **4.** _____ tremendously helpful for businesses. Organizing clients' appointments and files becomes a cinch.

5. _____, if you don't have the time or energy to run out to the neighborhood greeting card store to buy that special get-well card for a loved one, you can just log onto the computer and create an original, heartwarming greeting yourself.

6. _____, computers are helpful 24 hours a day, seven days a week.

7. _____, computers can also provide hours of amusement and enjoyment. **8.** _____, you can surf the Internet for the latest articles on fashion, sports, or movie stars. **9.** _____ enjoyable activity is to take your favorite CD, pop it into the computer, and sing the hours away! **10.** _____, the computer houses a vast collection of video games with amazing details and graphics that can entice you into playing for hours. **11.** _____, a typical boring day can just fly by when you are sitting at your PC and everything is just a click away.

A List of Transitions

To Show Place or Location	above, across, adjacent to, around, behind, below, beside, beyond, closer to, far from, nearby, opposite to, over, to the left, to the right
To Show Time	after, as soon as, before, during, earlier, immediately, in the future, later, meanwhile, soon, until, when
To Show Sequence	again, finally, first, next, second, soon, subsequently, then, third
To Show Similarities	in the same way, in the same manner, like, likewise, similarly
To Show Differences	although, but, even though, however, in contrast, nevertheless, on the other hand, otherwise, whereas, yet
To Add Information	again, also, another, furthermore, in addition, moreover
To Show Cause and Effect	as a result, because, consequently, for this reason, since, therefore, thus
To Introduce Examples	for example, for instance, in fact, to illustrate
To Conclude or Summarize	as a result, finally, in conclusion, in brief, in summary, therefore

CHAPTER 3

The Personal Narrative Essay

Background Information

When the Department of Education instituted the Pennsylvania State Writing Assessment, which includes narrative, informational, and persuasive writing, I taught the narrative essay first. However, now I begin with informational writing because of the unique structure inherent in personal narratives. Rather than following the regular, definable patterns of the informational or persuasive essay, a personal narrative tells a story about an individual experience, situation, or event or a "proposed occurrence at a particular time in a particular place." (Pennsylvania Department of Education/Division of Evaluation and Reports, 2001–2002, p.8) Another reason that I used to begin with the personal narrative rather than the informational essay is that initially I thought students would have an easier time writing about themselves. Wrong! Surprisingly, many of their personal accounts were dull, boring, and lifeless. Consequently, after I teach students about the structure of the narrative essay, I engage them in revision activities similar to those included in this chapter to help them add detail, color, and description to their writing.

Mini-Lesson	Writing Personal Narrative Essays
Objective	To model a personal narrative essay
	To generate a list of the characteristics of the personal narrative essay
	To prewrite, draft, revise, and edit a five-paragraph personal narrative essay
Time	One to three 40-minute class periods

Materials

- an overhead transparency and photocopies of the Personal Narrative Essay Model (page 50)
- photocopies of the Personal Narrative Essay Editing Sheet (page 52)

Step-by-Step

❶ Write the phrase *narrative essay* on the board. Challenge students to define narrative writing and provide examples of it. Differentiate between a personal narrative essay and a fictional short story. Ask students to discuss some of the similarities and differences between the two.

❷ Make and distribute a copy of the prompt below or write it on the board. Again, I link my prompts to the literature we are currently studying. In this case the class has just finished reading "The Necklace" by Guy de Maupassant. Read the prompt out loud to students and have them note the key words. Also, challenge them to state the topic and purpose of the prompt (topic: making a decision; purpose: to show the consequences of the decision).

The Prompt

In "The Necklace" by Guy de Maupassant, Madame Loisel and her husband make a fateful decision. They deliberately choose to be dishonest, and the consequences of their decision haunt them for a decade.

Like Madame and Monsieur Loisel, all of us are required to make decisions and choices in our lives.

Describe a time or event in your own life in which you were faced with making a decision or a choice. Show the consequences of your decision.

---

❸ Show the essay model "Promises Are Not Meant to Be Broken" on the overhead projector. Read it out loud, and use it to elicit the characteristics or features of narrative writing from students. Write their responses on the board or on chart paper. Guide them to discover that a five-paragraph personal narrative essay has the following characteristics:

- tells a story about a personal experience, situation, or event that occurs in a specific place at a specific time;

- uses some story elements, such as setting, plot, and characters;

- has a central or controlling idea that makes a point or conveys a message;
- includes an introduction with an attention-getting opening sentence, provides background information about the topic or experience, and contains a modified thesis statement in the last sentence that conveys the main idea of the essay;
- contains three body paragraphs;
- has an effective ending or conclusion that can sometimes reveal what the narrator has learned, provide food for thought, or create a powerful image or feeling;
- is usually told from the writer's, or first-person, point of view;
- is often arranged in chronological or sequential order;
- uses sensory detail, precise language, and some dialogue.

Note: As students compile a list of characteristics for each kind of essay, I jot down the title of the essay type at the top of a piece of chart paper. Then I add the features that students have come up with and post the list. Every time we focus on one of the essay types, I hang up the chart paper, which I have laminated, so that students can review that essay's particular characteristics.

❹ Have students individually brainstorm a list of situations in which they had to make an important decision. Some examples my students have used are whether or not to join a team, put an animal to sleep, attend a new school, disobey a parent, and get a job. By this time, students should be able to construct a Rule of Three web for their essay (see Mini-Lesson 4, page 12). If they need assistance, use the ideas in the model essay to help them. Again, instruct them to draft their essay.

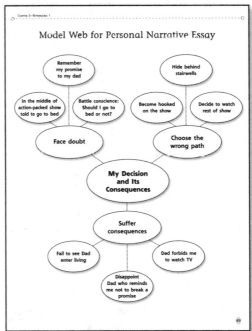

❺ When students complete their drafts, divide them into pairs or into groups of three or four. After distributing copies of the Personal Narrative Essay Editing Sheet, instruct group members to use the handout to edit each other's essay. Before beginning, you may want to spend some time explaining the various guidelines presented on the editing sheet.

A Revision Strategy for Adding Detail

Often my students' personal narratives lack vitality and description. For example, in one such essay Cassie writes about the struggles she endured when joining the softball team. After discovering she was the worst player on the team, Cassie practiced diligently and improved tremendously. However, as this award-winning writer describes the momentous occasion of receiving the Most Improved Player award at the team picnic, she writes,

> It warmed my heart to learn others understood my
> struggle and were impressed with my success.
> They were proud of me.

Even the best authors benefit from strategies that teach them how to enhance their writing style. Instead of becoming discouraged by flat description in your students' writing, seize the opportunity to teach a revision strategy. The following is a variation of Laura Harper's snapshots revision strategy described in the March 1997 issue of *Language Arts*.

❶ Write Cassie's quotation (see above) on the board or use a passage by a former student that lacks colorful details. Set the stage for the context of the quotation. In this case, explain that to overcome the obstacle of being the worst player on the team, Cassie spent countless hours practicing in the batting cage and throwing and catching with her brother. Then, in a critical game, with a runner on third, two outs, and the team down by a run, Cassie smacked the ball. The player on third base streaked down to home plate, and Cassie's team triumphantly won the game! As a result, she earned the Most Improved Player award. The quotation above described her feelings as she received the award.

❷ Next, have students zero in on the action of Cassie receiving the Most Improved Player award. Discuss some of the details Cassie could have included to show the thrill of the moment. Then, using some of the details discussed, have students create a cartoon frame and draw a picture of Cassie receiving the award. Ask students to write a two- or three-sentence caption describing the picture, as illustrated below.

My teammates, coach, and parents smiled broadly as I accepted the gleaming, gold Most Improved Player award. I really felt as if my insides were about to burst.

③ Now instruct students to zoom in on one of the details in their first drawing and create a second picture that focuses on that single detail. For example, one student may choose to highlight the award recipient's face; another may choose to concentrate on the trophy; and a third may focus on the coach's face. Below the second picture, have students write a two- or three-sentence description that is similar to the one below.

Beaming with pride, my coach's face could barely contain his broad, wide smile. He was all pearly whites and dimpled cheeks.

④ Finally, have students draw a third picture, in which they zoom in even closer on a detail in the second picture. For instance, in the example above, the student may choose to focus only on the coach's smile as depicted below. Again, have students write a two- or three-sentence caption for this picture, as shown below.

The coach's smile stretched as wide as a watermelon slice, and his dimples folded back into his face like an accordion. His pride swallowed me up and enlarged my heart twofold.

⑤ After students share some of their drawings and captions, demonstrate how to use the process of focusing on a specific detail to revise Cassie's original passage. Use the one below or create your own.

Revision

As my coach presented me with the Most Improved Player award, his smile stretched as wide as a watermelon slice, and his dimples folded back into his face like an accordion. His pride swallowed me up and enlarged my heart twofold.

⑥ Challenge students to find a passage in their own personal narrative that needs further description. Have them follow the steps listed above to revise the passage.

Activities to Help Students Add Detail to Personal Narratives

• Instead of starting the writing process with a list, web, or outline, begin with a guided journal entry that relates to the topic of the narrative essay. For example, if students are writing about a time when they were required to make an important decision, have them think about decisions they have made in the past and choose one to focus on in their journal. As they write, prompt them to add detail to their entries by asking lots of questions similar to the following:

> Where were you when you made the decision? Were you inside or outside? What did the walls or landscape look like? What kind of furniture was in the room, or what kind of birds and trees did you see? What did you smell? Who was there? What were they wearing? What patterns and colors did you see on their shirt or dress? Describe their scent and their facial expressions. What shape were their eyes? What kind of eyebrows did they have? How did you feel as you weighed the pros and cons of your decision? What were your inner thoughts? What did your conscience say to you? Who influenced your thinking? What were they saying? Were your hands loose or balled up in fists? How did your stomach feel? Your knees?

After students finish the entry, have them highlight or underline details they can use in their essay. Encourage them to group relevant details together.

• Create several sensory word banks for the classroom. First put decorated shoe boxes that are labeled "Sight," "Sound," "Taste," "Touch," and "Smell" around the room. Then place pencils and index cards beside each box. As students read stories, novels, and class work, have them find powerful sensory words. When they encounter one, direct them to write it on an index card and place it in the appropriate box. Encourage students to use the word banks as a writing resource. When they have collected at least 20 cards, compile a list of all the words and distribute it to the class. Finally, remind students to pull out the list whenever they have a writing assignment. You might even try creating an entire sensory word wall.

• Instruct students to find four or five vivid verbs in the essay "Promises Are Not Meant to Be Broken" such as *leaped*, *plastered*, *seesawed*, *zip*, and *trickled*. Next, have them highlight the verbs contained in their drafts and change four or five of them to make them more descriptive. Ask volunteers to physically act out a pair of their verbs to show the change in meaning. For example, if they substituted the verb *meandered* for *walked*, tell them to walk and then to meander.

Model Web for Personal Narrative Essay

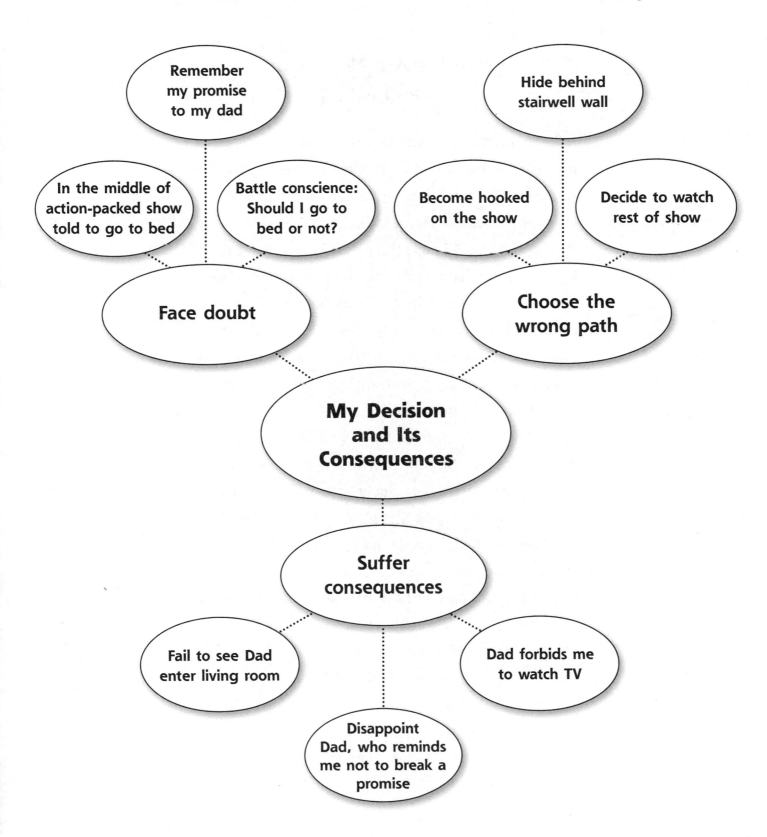

Personal Narrative Essay Model

Promises Are Not Meant to Be Broken

The anecdote, or "little story," in the introduction provides background information for the narrative essay. The last sentence is a modified thesis statement that outlines the three consequences of the decision.

My heart leaped with excitement! My hero (a.k.a. my dad) was taking care of my older brothers and me. At the very least, this meant chocolate marshmallow ice-cream cones and maybe even the privilege of staying up past 8:00 P.M. Clean, polished, and properly p.j.'d, I plastered my charming five-year-old smile on my face and politely begged to watch *Wagon Train*, a show that ended at 9:00, with my brothers. To my great delight Dad caved in but made me promise to go to bed at 8:30. Happily I crossed my heart and pledged to do as I was told. Little did I know that later I would face a decision that would fill me with doubt, cause me to disobey my dad, and lead me to suffer the unhappy consequences.

Along with *The Lone Ranger*, *Wagon Train* promised to become one of my favorite television shows. Filled with western frontier action, the trials and tribulations of America's early pioneers kept me and my siblings on the edge of our seats. Right in the middle of a dramatic showdown, my oldest brother told me it was 8:30, time for me to go to bed. Although a small voice whispered, "Remember what you promised Dad," a louder voice shouted, "Hide somewhere so you can see whether Cookie gets scalped!" Back and forth, up and down my conscience seesawed. Doubt clung to me like a wide strip of Velcro.

The first body paragraph relates to the first point of the modified thesis statement. It uses some dialogue, vivid verbs, and figurative language.

A clincher sentence summarizes the information.

The second body paragraph shows the narrator chooses the wrong path, the second point in the modified thesis statement.

"Bang!" The battle against the Indians began, and I was hooked. Pretending to head toward bed, I stealthily crept behind the stairwell wall. From there I had a clear view of the television, yet no one in the living room could see me. Propped up against the wall with my teddy bear in hand, I made my fateful decision: I would watch the rest of the show.

Totally enthralled by the action, I failed to see my dad enter the living room and head toward the stairs. Before I could zip into my room, Dad, red-faced and angry, appeared at the bottom of the steps. With a quivering voice he declared, "Sue, you must never, ever break a promise. I counted on you to keep your word." Immediately the tears welled up and trickled down my cheeks. I had disappointed my hero, and, even worse, I had disappointed my best moral self. Slowly my father continued, "I think an appropriate punishment would be to go without watching TV for an entire week. And that means no *Wagon Train*!" In the end, the prospect of not seeing any of my favorite shows did not bother me nearly as much as the thought of letting down my dear old dad.

The third body paragraph illustrates the consequences of the narrator's decision, the third point in the modified thesis.

The conclusion shows what the narrator learns from making her decision.

When I was just five I learned a valuable lesson from an extraordinary teacher: my dad. After disobeying him one night and suffering the natural consequences of my actions, I realized how important it is to keep a promise. To this day if I promise to do something, you can bet your bottom dollar that I will do it.

Name _____   Date _____   Section _____

Personal Narrative Essay Editing Sheet

Yes   No   **Focus**

___   ___   Does the story clearly relate to the essay topic?

___   ___   Does each detail and paragraph relate to the topic?

___   ___   Are there any sections, parts, or sentences that need to be removed
              because they do not relate to the topic?

ORGANIZATION
Introduction

___   ___   Is there an attention-getting opening?

___   ___   Does the introduction include background information about the topic?

___   ___   Is there an identifiable main idea or modified thesis statement in the
              last sentence of the introduction? Remember, in a narrative essay the
              writer may not be able to outline the three points.

___   ___   Does the introduction work? Does it relate to the body of the essay?

Body

___   ___   Are there at least three paragraphs?

___   ___   Does each body paragraph develop one main idea presented in
              the introduction?

___   ___   Are the paragraphs arranged in a logical order?

___   ___   Does one sentence relate to another?

___   ___   Are there smooth transitions between paragraphs? Does one paragraph
              flow into another?

___   ___   Are there transition words? (Circle these.)

Conclusion

___   ___   Does the conclusion/ending effectively and naturally end the narrative essay?

___   ___   Does the conclusion show what was learned, stimulate additional thought,
              or pack a powerful punch?

Mastering the Five-Paragraph Essay Scholastic Teaching Resources

Name _____ Date _____ Section _____

Yes	No	**Content**
____	____	Are there lots of specific details related to making the decision or choice?
____	____	Does the reader learn who, what, where, when, why, and how from the content?
____	____	Do the details paint a vivid, clear picture of what happened?
____	____	Is any dialogue or conversation used?

Usage (Conventions)

____	____	Are all sentences complete?
____	____	Is every paragraph indented?
____	____	Are all words spelled correctly?
____	____	Is proper capitalization used?
____	____	Is punctuation correct?
____	____	Is the grammar correct?

Style

____	____	Does the story sound serious, amusing, or frightening? In other words, can you identify a tone or mood?
____	____	Are the sentence beginnings varied? (Highlight the first four words of ten sentences to check this.)
____	____	Do you know how things look, feel, and sound? Are your five senses involved in the story?
____	____	Are the sentence lengths varied (short, medium, and long)?
____	____	Are there powerful adjectives? (Highlight at least four.)

CHAPTER 4

The Persuasive Essay

Getting Started

At this point students have had three experiences writing five-paragraph essays. Because they are now familiar with the basic structure of the essay, I approach persuasive writing a bit differently.

Mini-Lesson	**Writing Persuasive Essays**
Objective	To discover the characteristics of persuasive essays To state a position and support it with relevant facts, statistics, and examples To prewrite, draft, revise, and edit a five-paragraph persuasive essay
Time	Three to five 40-minute class periods
Materials	• persuasive writing topic cards (see below) • six to eight sheets of 18- by 12-inch construction paper • chart paper • markers • an overhead transparency and photocopies of the Persuasive Essay Model (page 59) • photocopies of the Persuasive Essay Editing Sheet (page 60)

Step-by-Step

❶ Prepare six to eight persuasive writing topic cards. For each card, simply jot down a subject that invites debate on a piece of 18- by 12-inch construction paper. Hang these up in various locations around the room.

Below are examples of topics I have used in the past:

- Should students be required to wear uniforms?
- Should there be year-round school?
- Should hunting be allowed?
- Should students be required to pass state tests in order to graduate from high school?
- Should the driving age be raised to 18?
- Should skateboards, bicycles, and scooters be banned from public places?
- Should school officials be allowed to conduct random locker and backpack searches?

❷ Tell students that they will be responding to one of the questions they see posted around the room. After reviewing the questions with the class, instruct students to move silently to the topic of their choice by the time you count to ten.

❸ Once the groups are in place, subdivide them into two sections based on their opinion about the topic. For example, students who are in favor of school uniforms form the first subgroup. Those who are against school uniforms form the second subgroup. Adjust group sizes if necessary; include no more than four students in each subgroup.

❹ After distributing chart paper and a marker to each group, have students appoint a team leader, whose job is to write down their topic along with their opinion, as illustrated below.

Students Should Have to Wear Uniforms

1.

2.

3.

Next, have the group brainstorm and list as many reasons as they can to support and defend their position. Ask them to circle their three strongest arguments.

❺ Because an important part of persuasive writing is developing convincing arguments that counter the other side's position, have students from the two subgroups share their ideas with each other. If there is only one subgroup, have those students use a second piece of chart paper to compile several persuasive arguments the other side might use to support its position.

⑥ Tell students that they are going to use the lists they have compiled to write a persuasive essay. Explain that they must now determine the audience to whom they will address their argument. Ask questions such as *To whom will you write to express your opinion about school uniforms? To ban hunting?* Generate a list of possible audiences and write it on the board. Have groups choose an appropriate audience for their topic and write it on the chart paper. Below are some of the audiences my students have selected in the past:

— the school board

— the principal and/or superintendent

— the mayor or board of county/township supervisors

— a state or federal representative or senator

— the editor of a local newspaper

⑦ Tell students that they now have everything they need to construct a persuasive essay. On the board draw a blueprint of the Rule of Three web (see Mini-Lesson 4, page 12), as depicted below.

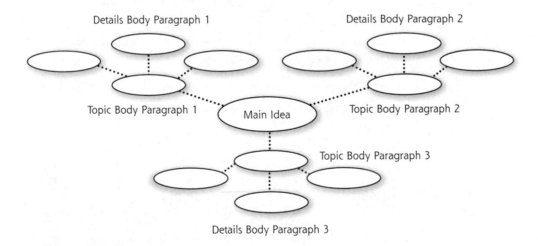

⑧ Instruct students to construct their webs on notebook paper and to use color coding. Tell them to place the topic, position, and audience written on the chart paper in the center of the web. In turn, the three reasons they circled become the three topics radiating from the center of their web. The supportive details include specific evidence, such as facts, examples, and statistics, that strongly supports each argument. Allow students to work individually or in groups to create the supportive details for their web.

⑨ After students have completed their webs, show the Persuasive Essay Model on the overhead projector. Then distribute copies to students. Through questioning, lead the class to understand the following characteristics of the persuasive essay:

- The Introduction
  - One way to begin is to consider some of the arguments raised by the opposing side in the first two sentences and then powerfully counter them in the third sentence.
  - The thesis statement clearly and directly states the writer's position and briefly outlines three reasons to support it.
- The Body
  - Each body paragraph develops one specific argument to support the writer's position. The writer selects reasons that consider and attempt to refute the opposing side's arguments.
  - Each body paragraph uses supportive details, such as facts, statistics, and examples, to increase the power and validity of the argument.
  - Smooth transitions are used within and between paragraphs to provide unity and coherence.
- The Conclusion
  - The ending restates the writer's position and summarizes the arguments and evidence presented in a powerful new way.
  - It has a strong, convincing tone.

⑩ Provide sufficient time for students to write their rough draft as well as to peer edit using the Persuasive Essay Editing Sheet as a guide. To assess the quality of their finished product, adopt the Rubric for a Five-Paragraph Essay (page 28). I explain to students that to earn a 4 in the content area they must have three strong arguments to support their position.

Revision Strategy: Style

Because powerful language plays such a vital role in persuasive essays, this is an excellent time to have students examine their own style. To begin, review a few stylistic elements of "Banning Recreational Vehicles in Public Places" (page 59).

- Have students identify several descriptive verbs used by the writer. List some on the board. Ask, *What effect do these verbs have on the reader? How do these verbs help the writer support his or her arguments?*

- Ask students to locate powerful adjectives. List some on the board. Ask what effect these have on the reader and why adjectives are important in persuasive writing.

- Have students find sentences, words, and phrases that have a strong, convincing tone. As they share their findings, instruct them to underline these word groups on their copy of the model.

- Ask students what kind of sentences the writer uses in this essay: interrogative, declarative, imperative, or exclamatory. Point out that although you do not want to overuse interrogative or exclamatory sentences, they can add power if used effectively. For example, sentence two in paragraph two might be more effective if it were a question: How many times have motorists slammed on their brakes to avoid hitting a skateboarder or a biker? Have students review their drafts and highlight a sentence or two that might benefit from this simple revision.

- Now distribute the reproducible Evaluating Style: A Revision Strategy (page 62). Encourage students to use it in revising the rough drafts of their persuasive essays.

Persuasive Essay Model

Banning Recreational Vehicles in Public Places

> The writer shows the harmless nature of the vehicles and then emphasizes their danger. This strengthens the power of the thesis and the writer's position.

At first glance skateboards, bicycles, and scooters appear to be harmless recreational vehicles. When these modes of transportation are operated in appropriate places, such as in skate parks or on bike trails, they can provide hours of pleasure and healthy exercise. However, when used in public places such as roads, sidewalks, and parking lots, they endanger society. Skateboards, bicycles, and scooters should be banned from such places to prevent injury, safeguard the public, and protect business owners from property damage and potential lawsuits.

The first reason to ban skateboards, bicycles, and scooters from inappropriate public areas is to protect people from being injured. For instance, as motorists back out of parking spaces at the mall, they are forced to slam on their brakes to avoid hitting a passing skateboarder or biker. Often drivers cannot see the individual who is operating the board or bike. Furthermore, enormous delivery trucks have the most difficult time discerning riders and can easily hit them, causing serious injuries and even death. Clearly, allowing skateboards, bicycles, and scooters to be operated in public places is dangerous.

> The topic sentences of the three body paragraphs state the reasons for the writer's position and relate back to the three points in the thesis statement. The supportive details use specific, realistic, powerful examples to develop each reason.

A second reason to ban these hazardous recreational vehicles is to safeguard the public. Skateboarders, bicyclists, and scooter riders can inflict harm on innocent bystanders. For example, an elderly woman, who has an arthritic hip and uses a cane to maneuver, was recently run down by a skateboarder who was using a handicap ramp to practice wheelies. Luckily, her injuries were not serious enough to require hospitalization; however, she was badly traumatized, shaken, and bruised. This incident poignantly demonstrates the need to prohibit these perilous vehicles from being operated in places where people walk, shop, or drive.

A third reason skateboards, bicycles, and scooters should not be permitted in heavily trafficked areas is that they can damage property and promote lawsuits. Recently at a local mall a skateboarder lost control of his board, which veered off the sidewalk and shattered a store window. Moreover, the flying shards of glass injured two customers. Consequently, the injured parties are suing the store owners for hundreds of thousands of dollars. If the injured parties win the suit, the store goes out of business, which further weakens the economy. Thus, the extensive damage these vehicles cause proves that they must be banned from inappropriate places.

> The conclusion begins with a restatement of the position. Powerful language and images are used to restate the reasons that support the position.

Allowing skateboards, bicycles, or scooters in areas open to the public is absolutely ludicrous! The riders easily could be killed by a car or truck. Moreover, young and old alike can be battered and bludgeoned by the vehicle operators who do not pay attention to where they are going. Finally, accidents caused by these recreational hazards can put store owners out of business. In summary, we should ban skateboards, bicycles, and scooters from inappropriate public places because they are a menace to society and can cause bankruptcy and death.

> The clincher drives the writer's point home.

Name _____   Date _____   Section _____

Persuasive Essay Editing Sheet

Yes   **No**   **Focus**

____   ____   Are the writer's topic and position clear?

____   ____   Does every paragraph develop a reason or argument to support
the position?

____   ____   Is each reason carefully developed?

____   ____   Do all sentences and paragraphs support or develop the position?

Organization

____   ____   Does the introduction powerfully draw the reader into the
writer's argument?

____   ____   Does the thesis statement clearly state the writer's position?

____   ____   Does the thesis statement briefly outline the reasons for the position?

____   ____   Does the paper have at least three paragraphs?

____   ____   Does the body develop three reasons for the position and give facts and
examples to support the position?

____   ____   Are there transition words? (Circle these.)

____   ____   Does the conclusion restate the position?

____   ____   Does the conclusion powerfully summarize the reasons in a new,
effective way?

Content

____   ____   Does the essay include a definite position on the issue?

____   ____   Are there strong reasons in support of the position?

____   ____   Do the facts and examples strengthen and support the position?

____   ____   Is the argument convincing?

Mastering the Five-Paragraph Essay Scholastic Teaching Resources

Name _____ Date _____ Section _____

Yes	No	**Usage (Conventions)**
____	____	Are all sentences complete?
____	____	Is every paragraph indented?
____	____	Are all words spelled correctly?
____	____	Is proper capitalization used?
____	____	Is the punctuation correct?
____	____	Is the grammar correct?

Style

____ ____ Does the writer use a strong, forceful voice that sounds clear and convincing?

____ ____ Does the writer use powerful, persuasive language?

____ ____ Are there a variety of sentence beginnings?

____ ____ Are there some short, medium, and long sentences?

Revision

Add something

Remove ~~the~~

Move

Substitute friendly ~~nice~~

Proofreading Symbols

¶	indent	✗ or **lc**	lowercase
a	capitalize	[ ] **R.O.**	(run-on)
∧	insert punctuation	[ ] **S.S.**	(sentence sense)
sp	spelling	[ ] **Frag.**	(fragment)

Name _____   Date _____   Section _____

Evaluating Style: A Revision Strategy

Directions: Choose <u>one</u> paragraph in your five-paragraph essay and do the following:

1. Highlight the first four words of each sentence. Examine the sentence beginnings.

Do the sentence beginnings vary?   **Yes   No**

If not, what can you do to improve them? _____

_____

Now make these revisions on your paper.

2. Circle all of your verbs. Put a check mark above the ones that need to be strengthened. Change these.

How many action verbs do you have? _____ How many linking verbs? _____

If there are too many linking verbs, make appropriate revisions.

3. Underline your adjectives in pen. Change the ones that you think need to be more powerful.

4. Count the number of words in each sentence. Write the number of words in the appropriate space below:

Sentence 1 _____   Sentence 2 _____   Sentence 3 _____   Sentence 4 _____

Sentence 5 _____   Sentence 6 _____   Sentence 7 _____   Sentence 8 _____

Evaluate your data. Do you have some short, medium, and long sentences?   **Yes   No**

Where should you change the sentence length? How should you change it?

Now make the necessary revisions on your paper.

5. Examine the kinds of sentences you use.

How many are declarative? ____ Imperative? ____ Interrogative? ____ Exclamatory? ____

How many are simple? ____ Compound? ____ Complex? ____ Compound-complex? ____

Evaluate your data. If necessary, revise some of your sentences to add variety.

Assess your style. What do you do well? What do you need to improve?

(Answer on the back. Use paragraph form.)

CHAPTER 5

Writing Across the Curriculum: A Compare-Contrast Essay

Getting Started

Being a science teacher has always seemed like a fascinating job to me. In science labs across the country, students and teachers observe, breed, and reproduce creatures as mysterious and mesmerizing as the praying mantis and the walking stick. Why not integrate language arts and science in order to share the fun and write across the curriculum? The model essay for this lesson is based on a classroom in which students actually observe these two resident creatures. Moreover, the teacher provides additional information about the praying mantis and the walking stick that students record in their notes. Often research becomes an integral component of the compare-contrast essay. Then sources need to be properly cited and documented. The resources I used for the model essay appear at the end of this chapter. Not only can you adapt the process outlined here to compare and contrast any two items in a variety of subject areas, but you can also use the model to introduce any compare-contrast essay.

As my students will tell you, this type of writing is difficult to structure. The two predominant ways of organizing the compare-contrast essay are the block method and the alternating method. In the first type, all the information about one item (the praying mantis) is presented, followed by all the points of comparison for a second item (the walking stick), as illustrated below.

     I. Introduction

    II. The praying mantis
       A. Appearance
       B. Behavior
       C. Method of reproduction

   III. The walking stick
       A. Appearance
       B. Behavior
       C. Method of reproduction

   IV. Conclusion

In the alternating method of organization, the writer presents a point about one item (the praying mantis's appearance) and then compares and contrasts it with the second item (the walking stick's appearance), as shown in this outline.

I. Introduction

II. Appearance
   A. Praying mantis
   B. Walking stick

III. Behavior
   A. Praying mantis
   B. Walking stick

IV. Method of reproduction
   A. Praying mantis
   B. Walking stick

V. Conclusion

Although I have taught both types of organization, my students and I prefer the alternating pattern. Consequently, I use this method in the model essay and structure prewriting activities that are compatible with this organizational framework, including the Compare-Contrast Graphic Organizer (page 69).

Mini-Lesson Writing Compare-Contrast Essays

Objective
To discover the characteristics of a compare-contrast essay
To prewrite, draft, revise, proofread, and construct final copies of a five-paragraph compare-contrast essay.

Time
Three to five 40-minute class periods

Materials
- an overhead transparency of the Compare-Contrast Essay Model (page 68)
- photocopies of the Compare-Contrast Graphic Organizer (page 69)
- photocopies of A List of Transitions (page 42)
- photocopies of the General Editing Checklist for Five-Paragraph Essays (page 27)

Step-by-Step

❶ Challenge the class to define the terms *compare* and *contrast*. Then decide which two things, such as the praying mantis and the walking stick, you are going to write about, or let students choose what they want to compare and contrast.

❷ Have students examine all the information they have about their two items, such as class notes, textbooks, field notes, and drawings. As a class, decide on three points of comparison, such as appearance, behavior, and method of reproduction. Always make sure that there is a sufficient amount of information to develop each point.

❸ Have students use the Compare-Contrast Graphic Organizer to structure their information. An example of a completed organizer appears below.

Points of Comparison and Contrast	Praying Mantis	Walking Stick
Appearance	Eyes: two compound; sees images and color; three simple Body: three parts: head, thorax, abdomen; exoskeleton; wings Legs: six; crab-like pinchers with sharp spikes for grabbing prey; fast	Eyes: two compound; sees images and color; three simple Body: three parts: head, thorax, abdomen; exoskeleton; no wings Legs: six; long; spindly; two claws and four suction-cup-type feet; helpful in climbing
Behavior	• can stay still for hours but moves faster than the eye can see when catching its prey • violent: predator; carnivore: eats cockroaches, grasshoppers, crickets; cannibalistic: offspring eat each other	• does not move much; long body makes it difficult to move; sways with tree branches; moves to eat, but is a herbivore; chews leaves slowly • docile: is not predatory; does not harm anything
Method of Reproduction	• mate in fall; afterward, female eats male • lays eggs: encased in sticky substance; cling to twigs, trees, and plant stems; hatch in spring	• reproduce in fall; female produces clone of herself through parthenogenesis • lays eggs: drop like seeds and scatter; hatch in spring

For each point of comparison, use two different colors to highlight noticeable similarities and differences in the items being compared. For example, use red to underline the similarities in the insect's appearance, such as compound eyes, three body parts, and six legs. Use blue to underline differences, such as pinchers, and two claws with four suction cups.

❹ On the overhead projector, show students body paragraph one from "Stranger Than Fiction: The Praying Mantis and the Walking Stick." Point out that the topic sentence relates to the first point of comparison, appearance, because that is the main idea of the paragraph. Then explain how the paragraph relates to the graphic organizer and groups the similarities and differences, using transition words to connect them. Circle the transition words. Lastly, emphasize the clincher's job: It summarizes the main idea and leads into the next paragraph.

⑤ Provide ample time for students to draft the first body paragraph of their essay. Distribute A List of Transitions, pointing out the words that are helpful when comparing and contrasting various items.

⑥ Peer edit the drafts, using the following questions:

- Does the topic sentence clearly state the main idea?

- Are there three supportive details?

- Do the comparisons make sense, or are you scratching your head as you read them? Put a question mark (?) next to confusing parts. Put a diamond (◆) next to comparisons that are logical.

- Circle the transition words.

- Examine the clincher. Does it summarize the main idea of the paragraph? Does it lead into the next paragraph? Underline the words that lead into the next paragraph.

⑦ Repeat steps 3 and 4 to construct body paragraphs two and three.

⑧ Display the model introduction on the overhead projector. Note that it

- begins with a surprising statement that draws the reader into the essay.

- introduces the objects being compared (praying mantis, walking stick).

- makes a general statement about the relationship between the two objects being compared.

- ends with a three-point thesis statement (main idea: the two insects are similar and different; opinion: creatures are stranger than fiction; three points of comparison: appearance, behavior, method of reproduction).

Have students draft the introduction. Instruct them to use the three points of comparison as the three points of their thesis statement. Peer edit the introduction using the criteria outlined in Mini-Lesson 6 on page 15.

⑨ Show the conclusion of the model essay on the overhead. Point out that the first sentence restates the thesis and uses the phrase "bug-eyed aliens from outer space" to connect back to the introduction. The next three sentences summarize the main ideas in a new way. Finally, the clincher leaves the reader with a powerful thought or idea.

⑩ Peer edit the conclusions based on the criteria listed in Mini-Lesson 8 on page 18. Use the General Editing Checklist for the Five-Paragraph Essay (page 27) before students write their final copies.

Teacher Tip

Younger students often have a difficult time writing a compare-contrast paper. To accommodate their needs, ask them to write a four-paragraph essay. In the first body paragraph tell them to show the similarities between the two objects being compared. In the second paragraph have them write about the differences.

References Consulted for the Compare-Contrast Essay

Classroom Animals and Pets—Insects and Co.—Walking Sticks. (2002). Retrieved July 25, 2004, from http://www.teacherwebshelf.com/classroompets/insectsandco-walkingsticks.htm

Facklam, M. (1994). *The Big Bug Book.* Toronto, Ontario, Canada: Little, Brown

Forest Preserve District of Cook County. (1977, May 28). *The Praying Mantis and Walking Stick* (Nature Bulletin No. 643-A). Retrieved July 25, 2004, from http://www.newton.dep.anl.gov/natbltn/600-699/nb643.htm

Lyon, W. F. (2000). *Praying Mantis* (Ohio State University Extension Fact Sheet HYG-2154-02). Retrieved July 25, 2004, from http://ohioline.osu.edu/hyg-fact/2000/2154.html

Compare-Contrast Model Essay

Stranger Than Fiction: The Praying Mantis and the Walking Stick

Two tiny, bug-eyed aliens may be living in your backyard right now. Difficult to see because they blend naturally into their environment and bizarre-looking when closely observed, the praying mantis and the walking stick are fascinating insects. A careful inspection of these creatures shows that one is relatively harmless while the other is a vicious cannibal. Overall, these stranger-than-fiction insects have both similarities and differences in their appearance, behavior, and method of reproduction.

First, the praying mantis and the walking stick have startling appearances. Both have compound eyes that seem to pop out of their heads and both see clearly and in color. While the praying mantis has wings and the walking stick does not, the insects do have a similar three-part body structure consisting of a head, thorax, and abdomen. Although they each have six legs, the front legs of the praying mantis have crab-like pinchers with sharp spikes to grasp its prey while the walking stick has two claws and four suction pads on its feet to aid in climbing. Even though the praying mantis and the walking stick have similar eye and body structures, their behavior differs dramatically.

Examining the actions of the praying mantis and the walking stick clearly indicates that one is naughty and the other is nice. Interestingly, the insects have one common characteristic: Both can remain still for hours. However, the praying mantis moves faster than the eye can see when it attacks its prey, while the walking stick wobbles because its elongated body prevents it from moving quickly. In addition, the carnivorous praying mantis exhibits violent predatory behavior as it slashes its living victims, such as crickets and grasshoppers; the herbivorous, docile walking stick, on the other hand, slowly and carefully chews a nearby leaf. Thus, the praying mantis is far more aggressive than the harmless walking stick, a characteristic that is also present in the insects' reproductive behaviors.

More differences than similarities exist in the way the praying mantis and the walking stick reproduce. First, the female of both species lays eggs in the fall; however, the female walking stick generally does not mate but reproduces clones of herself through a process called parthenogenesis. In contrast, the female and male praying mantis mate, but the wife devours her husband in a cannibalistic manner before he has a chance to scamper away! Another difference is that the eggs of the female walking stick drop like seeds and scatter to the ground, while the eggs of the praying mantis are encased in a sticky substance that clings to twigs, plant stems, and other objects. In sum, although both insects produce eggs in early fall, their mating habits and process of laying eggs differ dramatically.

In their appearance, behavior, and method of reproduction, the weird, wacky-looking praying mantis and walking stick certainly resemble bug-eyed aliens from outer space. Although their body structure is conventional, the praying mantis's vicious spiked claws and the walking stick's oversized, wobbly body make them stand out in a crowd. Behaviorally the two insects are almost polar opposites: The praying mantis acts like a psycho-killer, and the passive walking stick behaves like it is dead. When these insects reproduce, one species eats its mate while the other produces clones of itself. If you think that nothing strange ever happens in your backyard, slip on a pair of sneakers, grab a magnifying glass, and observe the stranger-than-fiction creatures that inhabit the trees, grass, and plants where you live.

Compare-Contrast Graphic Organizer

Points of Comparison and Contrast	Object 1:	Object 2:

CHAPTER 6

The Literary Essay: A Character Analysis

Getting Started

If surveyed, I believe the majority of middle and high school English teachers would agree that the most difficult part of the curriculum to teach is the five-paragraph literary essay. Marilyn Breed, an outstanding ninth-grade language arts teacher, definitely thinks so. Much of this chapter relies on her extremely helpful assignments on character analysis.

You will notice that this chapter is organized differently from the others. After suggesting strategies and tips about guiding students through the unique characteristics of a literary essay, I spell out the steps involved in teaching my first character analysis of the year. In the second half of the chapter, which focuses on common problems students have with the literary essay, I provide examples of how to address some of these issues.

Nine Strategies for Teaching and Writing Literary Essays

 **Strategy 1** Let students know in advance what the topic for their five-paragraph literary essay will be. After they have experience writing literary essays, allow them to choose their own subjects.

What I Do

The day students receive the novel *Fahrenheit 451* by Ray Bradbury, I explain that they will be writing a five-paragraph essay about the protagonist, Guy Montag, to show how he changes and develops over time.

Strategy 2 Have students collect information and data about the essay topic *as they read*, not after they have finished the novel.

What I Do

Each time I assign a portion of the book to read, I have students use a Reader's Response Journal to interact with the text. To help them collect their data for the character analysis, I require students to include a section in their response journal titled Analyze the Character. Because my students have seven journal entries for *Fahrenheit 451*, they have seven sections in which they have reflected about and analyzed the protagonist. Below are the directions I give students for this segment of the journal:

Analyze the Character

This section of the journal entry should be written in complete sentences. Record information you learn about Guy Montag by observing what he says, does, thinks, and feels; also record what you learn from his interactions with other characters. Pay particular attention to any changes you note in him. In your entry, list the page numbers on which you find important quotations that reveal information about Guy's character. Place a sticky-note next to these quotations so that you can refer back to them easily.

Strategy 3 Chunk the assignment into meaningful parts.

What I Do

Fahrenheit 451 is divided into three distinct segments. After students finish reading each section, I have them write a paragraph analyzing Guy Montag. For example, the topic of the first paragraph is to describe the protagonist at the beginning of the novel, focusing on his confusion and internal conflict. The topics for paragraphs two and three are to depict Montag as a man changing and to portray him as the new person that he eventually becomes. When students finish these assignments, the body paragraphs of the essay are essentially written.

Instead of using a web as the prewriting strategy, I require students to come up with an outline for each body paragraph, in which they write out the topic sentence. In addition, I encourage students to include short quotations as well as page numbers for the longer passages noted in the subsections of their outline. I also tell them that they may need more than three supportive details to prove their point. Below is the sample outline I share with my class.

Sample Outline

I. Introduction

II. In the beginning of *Fahrenheit 451* by Ray Bradbury, Guy Montag, an unhappy, confused individual, suffers from an internal conflict.
   A. Appears to be content with life and position as fireman
   B. Begins to wonder if firemen "ever put out fires instead of going to start them" (8)
   C. Questions morality of job and society after old lady's suicide (52)
   D. Realizes burning books is destructive

III. Guy Montag begins to change and to rebel against society.
  A. Begins reading books because "they can get us out of the cave" (76)
  B. Plans to plant books in firemen's houses and "turn in an alarm . . ." (85)
  C. Develops plan to illegally copy books
IV. Like the phoenix that is reborn from its ashes, Guy Montag symbolically destroys "his old self" and becomes an entirely new person.
  A. Burns house to ground
  B. Realizes he "must never burn again in his life" (141)
  C. Chooses to become a "book person"
  D. Transforms into a healer and leader
V. Conclusion

After demonstrating how to write the outline, I show students how to use it to construct their essay. I display the first paragraph of "The Evolution of Guy Montag" (page 77) on the overhead projector and carefully explain its relationship to the outline. While talking, I point out the basic rules for using quotations in literary essays:

Quotations should
  • flow naturally into the text and fit the context of the sentence and paragraph.
  • be brief (no more than three lines).
  • be enclosed in quotation marks. If you are directly quoting what a character says within a longer passage that is quoted from the text, use a quotation within a quotation (" ").
  • be followed by the page number in parentheses.

An ellipsis (three periods . . .) shows that words have been omitted.
Brackets [ ] indicate that the writer has inserted a word into the quotation.

I keep the rules simple and add to the list as needed. There are three other guidelines we review:
  • Do not use first and second personal pronouns in literary essays (*I, we, you*).
  • Use active verbs.
  • Use the present tense.

I continue by modeling paragraphs two and three and then challenging students to draft their own work. With a few minor adjustments, these paragraphs become the body of the five-paragraph character analysis.

Strategy 4 Provide peer and teacher feedback as students construct paragraphs.

What I Do

After students draft each paragraph, we edit and revise. I then collect and grade each paragraph. Although this may seem like extra work, it is well worth the time and effort. Because I can help correct any problems along the way, the second and third paragraphs improve and the final product becomes significantly better.

Strategy 5 Have students add the introduction.

What I Do

Because students have been creating outlines for the three body paragraphs as well as writing introductions to their essays all year long, this step is fairly straightforward. While showing a transparency of the introduction from the reproducible "The Evolution of Guy Montag," I emphasize that the first paragraph of a literary essay must contain the title of the work as well as the author's name. To craft the thesis statement, I tell students to think about the most significant aspect of Montag's character development and to use this as the main idea of their thesis. I also explain that to create the three points, all they need to do is abbreviate the three topics of their body paragraphs. When students complete their introductions, they are ready to peer edit.

Strategy 6 Demonstrate how to create transitions between the three paragraphs students have written.

What I Do

Because I write along with my students, I have typed copies of my own three paragraphs. Using these as a guide, I show the class how to revise the topic and clincher sentences, emphasizing the need for smooth transitions between the paragraphs. Below are some examples to teach this concept.

Original Topic Sentence—Body Paragraph 1	Revised Topic Sentence—Body Paragraph 1
In the beginning of *Fahrenheit 451* by Ray Bradbury, Guy Montag, an unhappy, confused individual, suffers from an internal conflict.	**In the beginning of the novel**, Guy Montag, an unhappy, confused individual, suffers from an internal conflict. **(Do not repeat the title and author; they appear in the introduction.)**
Original Clincher Sentence—Body Paragraph 1	**Revised Clincher Sentence—Body Paragraph 1**
In conclusion, Guy Montag's internal conflict fills him with doubt, anguish, and questions about his role as a fireman.	**Although** Guy Montag's internal conflict fills him with doubt, anguish, and questions about his role as a fireman, **he continues to move forward and gradually starts to change.** **(Makes a transition into Body Paragraph 2)**
Original Topic Sentence—Body Paragraph 2	**Revised Topic Sentence—Body Paragraph 2**
Guy Montag begins to change and to rebel against society.	**No longer certain of his identity**, Guy Montag begins to change and rebel against society. **(Connects to the clincher sentence in the previous paragraph, Body Paragraph 1)**
Original Clincher Sentence—Body Paragraph 2	**Revised Clincher Sentence—Body Paragraph 2**
In summary, Guy Montag transforms from a man who follows orders into a rebel who defies orders and society's laws.	In summary, as Guy Montag transforms into a rebel who defies society's laws, he is **on the road to becoming a new man.** **(Makes a transition into Body Paragraph 3)**

Strategy 7 Have students add the conclusion.

What I Do

Because the major components of the conclusion are similar to the ones in the other essays we have written, I simply model my conclusion on the overhead projector (see the reproducible "The Evolution of Guy Montag" on page 77) and review the salient features with the class.

Strategy 8 Do a final peer edit of the five-paragraph literary essay.

What I Do

I have pairs of students use the Literary Essay Editing Sheet (page 78) to correct each other's papers.

Strategy 9 Use a rubric to assess the final product.

What I Do

I continue to use the Rubric for a Five-Paragraph Essay (page 28) to evaluate student work; however, I tell the class that in order to score a 4 in organization and content they must have at least one quotation from the text in each body paragraph. In addition, the quotations must be properly introduced and interpreted.

Addressing Common Problems

Because of the extraordinary degree of higher-level thinking and writing skill involved in constructing a five-paragraph literary essay, students are bound to encounter some problems. Below are three common difficulties my students have and examples of how I address them.

Common Problem 1 The Thesis Statement

How I Address It

There are three basic problems that students encounter when trying to construct a coherent thesis. The statements are either too long, missing completely, or lacking one of the three components (main idea + opinion + three points). Over the years, I make a point of saving photocopies of student papers that have either excellent or problematic thesis statements. As an activity, I type these out, ask a series of questions about the examples, and challenge the class to revise the confusing statements. We share and discuss the revisions. Often I have students write the changes on the board, and we evaluate them together. At the top of page 79 are two student-generated thesis statements and questions I have the class answer about each one. These examples can be presented as an overhead transparency or as photocopies to be distributed to the class.

Common Problem 2 Weak Introductions and Conclusions

How I Address It

First, I type two examples of introductions or conclusions written by former students, including one that is excellent and one that needs improvement. Together we read the paragraphs, using questions I have composed to analyze them. In addition, I constantly share samples of effective introductions and conclusions both during the peer-editing process and after the essays have been evaluated. The more models students read, the better their introductions and conclusions become. On page 79 are two introductions, along with questions to help students evaluate them. The first one is missing the three-point thesis statement.

Common Problem 3 Ineffective Use of Quotations

How I Address It

Students experience a variety of problems as they learn how to incorporate quotations into the text. Two of the most common mistakes they make are using quotations without interpreting them and choosing a quotation that does not fit the context of the paragraph. They also have difficulty making the quotation fit comfortably into the text, usually because of a grammatical error. Again, I use student work to develop a separate activity for each issue. Often I put the problematic quotation on a transparency, and we identify and correct the mistake as a class. At the bottom of page 79 is a student essay that simply lists the quotes and an example of a class revision. Again, these examples can be presented on an overhead transparency or as photocopies to be distributed to the class.

Differentiating Instruction

For older or more advanced students, I require twelve to fifteen sentences in each body paragraph of the literary essay. To help students achieve this goal, they first generate formal topic outlines for each body paragraph. These outlines include three major points and three elaborative sub-points, as illustrated in the skeletal outline of a single body paragraph that appears at right.

I.
  A.
    1.
    2.
    3.
  B.
    1.
    2.
    3.
  C.
    1.
    2.
    3.

Character Analysis Model Essay
The Evolution of Guy Montag

Can one person alter the course of history? In the novel *Fahrenheit 451* by Ray Bradbury, Guy Montag's evolution as a character demonstrates that an individual can impact society. Initially, Montag experiences an internal conflict that motivates him to change. As he gradually transforms, he ultimately becomes a new person who rises above the tyranny of the majority. Throughout the novel **Montag's character grows** dramatically, **moving from a man in conflict** to a **man evolving**, until he ultimately **becomes a new and better person.**

In the beginning of the novel Guy Montag, an unhappy, confused individual, suffers from an internal conflict. Even though he burns people's books and homes to earn a living, he appears to be content with his life and his occupation as a fireman. However, after he meets Clarisse McClellan, he wonders if firemen ever "put out fires instead of going to start them" (8). He also admits he is not happy. Finally, after witnessing an old woman commit suicide because of her love for books, guilt-ridden Montag begins to question the morality of his society and his job when he observes that "it took a man a lifetime maybe to put some of his thoughts down, looking around at the world and life, and then I come along in two minutes and boom! It's all over" (52). For the first time Montag realizes that burning books is destructive and immoral. Although his internal conflict fills him with doubt, anguish, and questions about his role as a fireman, he continues to move forward and gradually starts to change.

Even though he is confused about his identity, Guy Montag begins to evolve and rebel against society. First, in his quest for truth and knowledge, he starts reading the books society outlaws, believing that "maybe books can get us half out of the cave . . . and keep us from making . . . insane mistakes" (76). Second, Montag and Faber, a former English professor, develop a plan to destroy the book-burning industry. The men plot to plant books in the firemen's houses, "turn in an alarm, and see the firemen's houses burn" (85). In addition to destroying the book burners, the two men also decide to contact an unemployed printer to help them make illegal copies of the forbidden books. In summary, as Guy Montag evolves into a rebel who defies society's laws, he is on the road to becoming a person who barely resembles his former self.

Like the phoenix that is reborn from its ashes, Montag symbolically destroys his "old self" and metamorphoses into an entirely new man. Ironically, he burns his own house, his pyre, to the ground, destroying all possessions, memories, and any semblance of the former Guy Montag, Fireman 451. As he leaves the city behind and floats down the baptismal waters of the river, he realizes why "he must never burn again in his life" (141). He chooses to become a "book person" who uses knowledge to teach people about the past to prevent them from repeating its horrific mistakes. Instead of destroying the world around him, Montag transforms into a healer, a leader who marches toward the bombed-out city to rebuild, rekindle the light of hope, recite the book of Ecclesiastes, and resurrect knowledge. Thus, as Montag rises from the ashes of his former self, he becomes an entirely new person destined to change the world for the better.

In conclusion, the transformation of Guy Montag from a man in conflict to a soulful intellectual is extraordinary. Riddled with doubt and guilt at the beginning of the novel, he emerges as a completely new persona. As he rises from the ashes and the funeral pyre of his first life, Montag evolves into a contemplative individual, a thinker whose sensitivity and biblical knowledge inspire others and create hope for mankind. Can one person change the course of history? With the touch of his hands and the memory of "Revelations" emblazoned in his mind, Montag leads the movement toward "the healing of nations" (167) and the restoration of life.

Name _____   Date _____   Section _____

Literary Essay Editing Sheet

| ✓ = everything is included | ✓– = needs work | 0 = not there |

The Introduction

_____ 1. Begins with an attention-getting sentence.

_____ 2. Includes the title of the novel and the author's name.

_____ 3. Briefly describes what the body of the paper will contain.

_____ 4. States the three-point thesis last. (Number the points and underline what the writer plans to prove in the paper.) Is three to five sentences in length.

_____ 5. Is about five sentences in length.

The Body Paragraphs

_____ 1. Have a topic sentence that relates back to the thesis.

_____ 2. Have three supportive details. (Number these.)

_____ 3. Contain one relevant quotation from the novel. The quotations are enclosed in quotation marks and page numbers are properly cited at the end.

_____ 4. Contain two or three transition words or phrases. These must be circled or typed in bold. (Circle them if the writer forgot to do so.)

_____ 5. Contain a clincher. This sentence often leads into the next paragraph and serves as a transition sentence.

_____ 6. Are linked by transitions that are evident and clear.

_____ 7. Contain a minimum of five sentences. (Count the sentences before you place a check mark in front of this item.)

_____ 8. Are clear, logical, easy to understand, and develop a single idea related to the essay topic.

Name _____   Date _____   Section _____

The Conclusion

_____ 1. Restates, or echoes, the thesis statement without simply repeating it.

_____ 2. Summarizes the major points.

_____ 3. Includes a detail or example from the introduction that ties up the essay.

_____ 4. Ends with a strong image or powerful statement.

_____ 5. Is about five sentences in length.

Usage (Conventions)

Yes	No	
___	___	Are all sentences complete?
___	___	Are all words spelled correctly?
___	___	Is proper capitalization used?
___	___	Is the punctuation correct?
___	___	Is the grammar correct?

Revision

Add   something ⌃

Remove   ~~the~~

Move   ⟲→

Substitute   friendly ~~nice~~ ⌃

Proofreading Symbols

¶	indent		⁄ or **lc**	lowercase
a (capitalize mark)	capitalize		[ ] **R.O.**	(run-on)
⌃	insert punctuation		[ ] **S.S.**	(sentence sense)
(sp)	spelling		[ ] **Frag.**	(fragment)

Mastering the Five-Paragraph Essay Scholastic Teaching Resources

Common Problem 1: The Thesis Statement

Student Example 1

In this novel, Guy Montag begins as a troubled, puzzled man who is becoming doubtful of the society in which he lives, then he begins to change, react, and become malleable to people and the forces around him, and finally Montag has become an entirely new man like when the phoenix becomes an entirely new phoenix as it rises from its ashes.

Student Example 2

Thus, Guy Montag undergoes several significant changes during the story and becomes an entirely different person.

My Questions

1. Underline the main ideas in thesis statements 1 and 2. Number three points in each statement.
2. What is the writer's opinion about Guy Montag in thesis statement 1? In thesis statement 2?
3. Why does the writer need to revise thesis statement 1? Thesis statement 2?
4. Revise and rewrite both thesis statements.

Common Problem 2: Weak Introductions and Conclusions

Student Example 1

In *Fahrenheit 451* by Ray Bradbury, Guy Montag goes from being the model citizen to being a criminal in one week. Montag changes his mind-set, and doing so changes the beliefs that he has cherished since childhood, and is reawakened to the immoral, book-burning society that he plays a large role in. Montag starts out thinking he is happy, but realizes that he is not. Then, as the book progresses, Montag begins to change. Finally, Montag completes his change and is reborn.

Student Example 2

Picture a society in which books are burned and any creative thinking results in a prison sentence. This is the society Ray Bradbury, author of *Fahrenheit 451*, has created for his protagonist Guy Montag, a man who goes through many changes. Initially, Montag is in constant conflict with himself and is immersed in shallow happiness and false relationships. Then he becomes a catalyst for change, and the winds of change blow him away to a land of new thoughts and opinions. Because Montag starts to think, he emerges from the ashes of his old life and becomes a new man. During the course of the novel, Montag evolves as he questions his values, begins to think for himself, and transforms into an intellectual and an individual.

My Questions

1. Which introduction is most effective? Why do you think that is so?
2. Which introduction needs to be improved? Why?
3. Rewrite and revise the introduction that needs improvement.

Common Problem 3: Ineffective Use of Quotations

Student Example

Guy reveals his confusion about his job when he states, "I'm lost without it," (80) and "Where do we go from here?" (76). "We have everything we need to be happy but we aren't happy. Something's missing" (84), his hunger for knowledge and his pursuit of individuality supersedes his doubt and uncertainty.

The Revision

Guy reveals his confusion about his job when he states, "I am lost without it" (80). **As he struggles to find a new career and way of life he ponders**, "Where do we go from here?" (76). **What he is certain about is his unhappiness:** "We have everything we need to be happy but we aren't happy. Something's missing" (84). **Ultimately, Montag threads his way through his inner turmoil and allows his desire for knowledge and his pursuit of individuality** to supersede his doubt and uncertainty.

Final Thoughts

Students wipe perspiration from their furrowed brows. And as I grade yet another set of five-paragraph essays I think, "Is it finally June?" Yes, writing organized, cohesive, and compelling essays demands time, energy, commitment, and patience. At times the experience can be frustrating; however, it is also exhilarating and rewarding.

As my students reviewed their writing at the end of the year, reflecting on what they learned and examining their strengths and weaknesses, I heard giggling and laughter. When I asked them why they were chuckling, Alexis spoke for her peers: "How did you put up with our writing at the beginning of the year? Even I can't understand what I wrote in my first literary essay. Boy, I can't believe how much I've improved!" Then we all laughed joyfully and triumphantly together, basking in the glory of our shared struggle and success, knowing that for one shining moment, we had collectively ignited the lamp of learning.

Bibliography

Harper, L. (1997). The writer's toolbox: Five tools for active revision instruction. *Language Arts, 74*(3), 193–200.

Jensen, E. (1998). *Teaching with the brain in mind.* Alexandria, VA: American Association for Supervision and Curriculum Development.

National Council of Teachers of English and International Reading Association. (1996). *Standards for the English language arts.* Newark, DE, and Urbana, IL.

Pennsylvania Department of Education Division of Evaluation and Reports. (2001–2002). *Writing assessment handbook.* Harrisburg, PA: Author.

Sprenger, M. (1999). *Learning and memory: The brain in action.* Alexandria, VA: American Association for Supervision and Curriculum Development.

Tomlinson, C. A., & Kalbfleisch, M. L. (1998). Teach me, teach my brain: A call for differentiated classrooms. *Educational Leadership, 56*(3), 52–55.

Web Resources

The Web sites listed below contain information about five-paragraph essays. They include sample prompts, student examples, and handouts.

Sites for Prompts

Informational/Expository	http://www.state.tn.us/education/tswritinge.htm
Narrative	http://members.accessus.net/~bradley/narrativeprompts2.html
Persuasive	http://home.earthlink.net/~jhholly/persuasive.html

Sites for General Information About Five-Paragraph Essays

http://cctc2.commnetedu/grammar/five_par.htm

http://grammar.ccc.commnet.edu/grammar/five_par.htm

http://depts.gallaudet.edu/EnglishWorks/writing/fiveparagraph.html